The Do's and Don'ts of
PARENT INVOLVEMENT

How to Build a Positive School-Home Partnership

Cathrine Kellison McLaughlin

Innerchoice Publishing

Copyright © 1993, Cathrine Kellison McLaughlin • All rights reserved
Revised Edition, 2011

ISBN – 10: 1-56499-075-4
ISBN – 13: 978-1-56499-075-4

INNERCHOICE Publishing
15079 Oak Chase Court
Wellington, FL 33414

www.InnerchoicePublishing.com

Surveys and other tools may be reproduced in quantities sufficient for use in organizing and maintaining parent-involvement and related programs. All other reproduction, for any purpose whatsoever, is explicitly prohibited without written permission. Request for such permission should be directed to
INNERCHOICE PUBLISHING

Acknowledgment

My three daughters grace me daily with their innate wisdom and patience, and I grow daily because of Joni, Jonna and Simone. They give me hope for the future of humanity, and Joni in particular inspires and humbles me with her own growth. My parents, John and Allie Clayton, bless me as living examples of enduring love and of humor in the hard times.

Many thanks go also to supporters like Lee Teitel, Beatrice Teitel, Joe McLaughlin, Susan Immergut, Susanna Palomares and Dave Cowan. The many parents I've learned from include Barkley and Ken Bonnaffons, Kathy Fung, Lily Gomez, Susan and David Irving, Rosemary Kassell, and Mariann Perseo. My inspiration to work hard on this book comes from illuminated educators like Lesley Gordon and Anthony Alvarado, as well as from the many researchers who dedicate their energies to being better parent educators.

I've saved the best for last: my deepest gratitude and affections go to Jeffrey, co-parent supreme, lifemate, and my best friend.

Cathrine Kellison McLaughlin

Contents

Introduction 1

Section One: Who Are Today's Parents 9

    Reaching Out to Culturally Diverse Parents 11

    What Makes an "Involved Parent?" 16

    Parent Enthusiasm Or Parent Burnout 18

    How Parent Involvement Benefits Schools 20

    Administrators Play a Crucial Role 23

    The Major Components of an Effective Parent-Involvement Program 26

    Starting a Parent-Involvement Program in Ten Steps 30

    What Are the Obstacles to Parent Involvement? 32

    The Great Rewards of Parent Involvement 37

    The Essential Elements of Parent Involvement 42

Section Two: Reaching Out! 45

    1. Reaching Out to Parents 46

    2. Keeping Parents Involved 62

    3. Gathering Information 73

    4. Conferences, Conversations and Home Visits 86

    5. Asking Parents to Volunteer at School 99

    6. Ideas for Social Gatherings, Projects, and Events 105

    7. Organizing Parent-Teacher Groups 135

    8. Forty-five Ways to Give Recognition to Volunteers 151

Section Three: Parents Reach Out: To the School, the Community, and Each Other 154

    The Children Are the Focus 156

    Ways That Parents Can Reach Out to Teachers 160

    Ways That Parents Can Reach Out to Each Other 163

Concluding Remarks 173

Sample Surveys, Letters, Bulletins, and Other Tools

    Who Is a Counselor?...54

    Hello Parents. We'd like to get to know you better!! 75

    Student and Parent: What Concerns You? 76

    Newsletter Survey 78

    Teachers' Questions for Parents 79

    A Student-Teacher-Parent Agreement 82

    Teacher's Commitment to the Family 83

    Teacher-to-Family Bulletin 84

    Parent-to-Teacher Bulletin 85

    Parent-Teacher Conference Guidelines 90

    Welcome to the Greenfield Elementary Parent-Teacher Conference 91

    I'm Excited About Meeting You! 92

    Questions the Parent Can Ask the Teacher in the Conference 93

    A Phone Call to the Child's Home: Suggested Script 98

    A Volunteer Checklist 102

    Community Volunteer Survey 103

    Teacher's Request for Classroom Volunteer 104

    Your PTA (membership recruitment letter) 142

There is no program or policy that can substitute for a mother or father who will attend those parent-teacher conferences or help with the homework or turn off the TV, put away the video games, and read to their child. Responsibility for our children's education must begin at home.

President Barack Obama
Addressing a joint session of Congress,
April, 2009

Introduction

Taking a Good Look at Parent Involvement

As a parent, I've worked in my daughters' public schools for 13 years. I feel good about trading my few hours of school volunteering for the many hours of good steady education my kids get. As a writer, I've looked through books on parent involvement and been excited by different ideas. As a member of a tight-knit New York City community, I know the children whose parents work closely with them and the school, and the children whose parents do not.

But it took one particular experience to fuel my decision to write *The Do's and Don'ts of Parent Involvement*.

My husband, younger daughters, and I recently bought an old country house high in the Adirondack Mountains. I had spent hours one day happily plowing through cupboards and closets with boxes of antique lace from the 20s and 30s, chintz aprons from the 40s, plastic shower curtains from the 50's, and — here comes the experience — three huge boxes of the most popular magazines from the 50s, 60s, and 70s.

I looked through over 200 of these magazines. When I was through, I had found only two articles on parenting. Two! Oh, there was a lot of special interest material, all right: how to please one's husband through his tummy, how to wear hair and apply makeup, holiday recipes, home decorating, even blushing hints on keeping love and sex alive. But there was virtually no parenting information or support, no guidelines, no encouragement. Our parents were essentially in the dark.

This helped me to see that today's parents have at least a fighting chance in comparison to our parents' generations. We have books, we have digital media, we have experts. And most importantly, we have allies in one another — educators, counselors, administrators, community groups, and most importantly, in fellow parents. We can explore and create strategies for parent involvement, and use our positive results to shape a new generation with our efforts.

The energy and positive intentions of parents hold extraordinary promise. Parents inherently possess great potential as powerful conduits to their children's academic and social and emotional growth, but are often abandoned by systems too overburdened, uninformed, or apathetic to use them well. And so they remain: an untapped resource.

The Do's and Don'ts of Parent Involvement provides the support and information needed to fill the void that keeps parents from becoming motivated and involved. The book talks directly to the parents, teachers, counselors and other people involved with children, from preschool through high school. It is written specifically for:

> **Parents and Families** — PTAs, PTOs, other parent-centered groups who realize that their contributions are vital to their child's success, and willingly make an on-going commitment to be actively involved.
>
> **Administrators** — who realize that the big picture is incomplete without the support of parents in their children's education.
>
> **Teachers** — who pledge their energy to work alongside parents and children in the classroom and in the home, using positive and collaborative methods to further the child's education.
>
> **Counselors** — who work closely and consistently with children and their families in furthering the educational and emotional capacities of children.

Community Groups — who encourage and support the ongoing efforts of the school, parents, families, and children to work together. These organizations include local businesses, agencies, community centers, churches, and neighborhood outreach programs.

Throughout the book, you will find sample survey forms, letters, memos, bulletins, and other valuable tools. You may be able to use some of these pages just as they are. In most instances, however, you will want to modify them to suit the needs of your school and parent group. In either case, please take advantage of the samples. They were developed for you.

Parenting Was Supposed to Just Come Naturally.

Thirty or forty years ago, most of what children learned about the world came to them from family and friends in social and religious settings. Television was influential then, as now; we learned from TV that the family was run by a white, middle class male who was patient, understanding — and always employed — and an unflappable mom who thrived in the kitchen and handled problems with wisdom. We were given a simple, uncomplicated view of the world we lived in.

Parents have read a "Keep Out" sign for years.

For decades, institutionalized education for the most part kept parents at bay. Just like television, educators gave parents a simple set of guidelines and seldom welcomed them to walk its hallowed halls. Their encouragement to parents was limited: help with homework, come to PTA meetings and school plays, cook for an occasional bake sale or pot luck dinner. And nothing more than that.

Even now, some educators feel that it's their duty to protect or separate children from what they see as unenlightened or inappropriate family influences. Recent surveys reflect the sad fact that despite today's more global outlook, this viewpoint isn't changing much. A poll of East Coast elementary school principals showed that most are comfortable keeping parents in traditional, well-defined roles in the school: helping with parties and class trips or talking in the classrooms about their interests, hobbies, or careers. These principals don't feel that parents have the proper skills to tutor children, or to help the teacher in more significant ways. However, the same principals admit that their teachers are not sufficiently trained to work effectively with parents. In the past, parents who were advocates for their child's education were seen as interfering trouble-makers, or as sadly misinformed and therefore impotent. The school humored parents, and hoped they'd go away.

But the times, they are a changin'...

Educators, schools, parents, and counselors are rapidly realizing that in these changing times, they need all the help they can possibly get, because:

- Students are graduating — barely — with few or no job skills.
- High school drop-out rates are rising, especially among low-income and minority youth.
- Families have multiple social and economic problems.
- The basic structure of the family is radically changing.
- Teen-age pregnancy rates are skyrocketing.
- Alcohol, drug, tobacco, and sexual abuse are worsening.
- Fewer funds for education-related needs are being allocated.
- Job stress and unemployment pressures are building.
- Domestic anguish, violence, and continual abuse invade families.
- Salaries no longer keep up with rising family costs.
- AIDS-related and catastrophic health care costs are exploding.
- Peer pressure is growing as peer groups exercise greater influence on kids lacking nurturing support at home.
- It's harder to make and maintain a strong home-school connection.

The demographics in America are changing, too:

- **Immigration.** There continues to be a large influx of immigrants into the country, due to political pressures, economic hardships, and failing global governments.
- **Minority growth.** Minority populations are growing. Right now, minority children will be taking their places at one out of every three desks in most classrooms.
- **Majority decline.** Birthrates are decreasing among whites, while the Hispanic population constitutes about 27 percent of the U.S. population

Where Are the Today's Parents?

The parents are here, and they do care. But, because both parents usually work or many are single parents, most are subject to new kinds of stress and competition unique in the history of the work place.

Parents who live in urban areas, and especially minority or low-income parents, have concerns about the school their child attends. These concerns are usually well grounded and often make parents feel helpless, frustrated and angry, or isolated and afraid.

These concerned parents want to know that:
- Their child is getting equal attention from the teacher and the school.
- The discipline their child receives at school is appropriate and not violent.
- Drugs are not a part of the school environment.
- The discipline they are giving their child is effective and appropriate.
- The teacher is able to tell them how and what their child is doing in school and will genuinely listen to their concerns.

- The teacher honestly cares for and empathizes with each child.
- Their child gets along with other children and adults.
- There are ways of getting information about how the school itself, and the education system in general, work.
- They as parents can improve their lives, and there are ways to get help for themselves, their family, and their child.

The future looks brighter.

Fortunately, the once-bleak outlook is changing. Schools are finally becoming aware that one extraordinary resource that often goes untapped is the energy and influence of parents. Parent involvement is available and effective. It's simply a matter of reaching out and mobilizing the players, and keeping parents' energies challenged and directed. It isn't always easy, but it's always possible.

Section One
Who Are Today's Parents?

Parents and families in the 21st century are a far cry from the traditional two-parent, happy homemaker romanticized version. Only seven percent of all American school-age children live in a home with two parents who are married to each other, only one of whom works outside the home.

On the other side of the spectrum, more than three quarters of mothers whose children are in school work outside the home. And, across all income and cultural lines, close to 25 percent of all children under eighteen live with only one parent. That translates to over 13-million single parents in America.

Today's family structures are diverse

- **Two-income:** fast-track stressed-out parents
- **Mother at home, father at work:** traditional, rare
- **Single parent:** divorced, widowed, adoptive, foster, step
- **Low-income, at-risk:** poverty, hold multiple jobs, troubled home, little time for homework help
- **Grandparent as parent:** unplanned second-time parenting, aging problems, cultural divides, yet often best choice
- **Gay parent:** single or in a couple relationship, face some hostility or misunderstanding, strong interest in child rearing

Growing, bearing, mothering or fathering, supporting, and at last letting go of an infant are powerful and mundane creative acts that rapturously suck up whole chunks of life.
—Louise Erdrich

- **Step-parent:** part- or full-time with spouse's kids, often each parent brings kids into relationship
- **Foster parent:** through government or private system
- **Adoptive parent:** single, married, or domestic partners choose adoption, often from other cultures or races
- **Multicultural parent:** color, culture, race, religion all factor into this group which is rapidly expanding in our multi-cultural society

Today's parents feel less capable of helping

Almost a quarter of all employed parents encounter problems at work if they have to leave due to a school activity, stay home to care for a sick child, attend a parent-teacher conference, or receive calls at work from their child. Parents often think of themselves as unable to help with school work. A small majority (58 percent) feels competent enough to help their child in three classic subjects: math, English and history. Fewer parents feel confident assisting with science and computers.

Today's parents want more

Today's parents want to spend more time with their child. They worry that their child is growing up alone and untended. At the same time, parents want more out of their own lives than the preceding generation. Today's parents think more about philosophical and spiritual fulfillment, and at the same time want more tangible goods. Today's parents are less likely to live through their child, and want a fuller life than their parents had. The tug of war between one's own needs and the needs of the child is a challenge to parents, and calls for extra skills to handle the conflicts that arise.

Reaching Out to Culturally Diverse Parents

America's unique population

The faces of America reflect myriad colors, cultures, and languages. The richness of cultures and ethnic backgrounds collectively form, and continually change and challenge, the spirit of our country. The American Dream attracts and tantalizes — but not without a price. Our cultural melting pot threatens to eradicate ethnic customs, language, and background. The strain on city, state, and federal budgets to educate the immigrant and second-generation population is enormous. Many students have difficulties with academics, and with mastering the language. The drop out rate is rising. The fact that there's a shortage of skilled labor is reluctantly being acknowledged by the private sector but little is being done to counteract it. Many children leave school under-educated and uninspired, often not joining the workforce but hitting the unemployment lines instead.

The population changes

In 2009, according to the U.S. Department of Education, our student population looked like this: Caucasians were still the majority, comprising almost 54% of the student population. African-Americans were at 17%, Latinos 22%, and Asians and others number 7%. The homosexual population has not been accurately predicted, and other culturally diverse groups might overlap some of the above.

This expanding rainbow of students and parents cannot continue to radiate without guidelines. School is one of the few places in which people from different backgrounds can create a successful and life-long collaboration.

The barriers grow higher.

When parents arrive in our country, or, if they are second- or third-generation people who have not mastered English or useful skills for better employment, they are barraged by strange and often intimidating barriers that preclude their getting involved in their child's educational growth.

Cultural challenges for some parents:

- There's no existing family tradition of direct involvement in the education of one's child.
- They use body language as communication tools, such as avoiding direct eye contact.
- They need more flexibility to schedule meeting times with the teacher.
- They think teachers should demand and get respect from students and be in control.
- They need more information on helping their child with homework, discipline, health and nutrition, but they don't know how or who to ask.
- They can't comprehend the extent of learning disabilities or handicaps in their child and/or don't know how to pursue resources and help.
- Non-English-speaking parents often have a different or non-expressive communication style that English-speaking people misinterpret.
- Non-English-speaking parents look up to the teacher as the respected authority. This makes it difficult for the parents to express their candid opinions or genuine concerns.
- The school's culture often differs considerably from that of the home.

Language barriers for some parents:

- English-speaking educators often have trouble understanding the real needs and concerns of non-English-speaking parents and vice versa.
- Non-English-speaking parents tend to be more hesitant during parent-teacher conferences to speak their true feelings or needs.
- Many parents find it very difficult to understand the inner workings of the educational system in general, and their child's school system in particular.
- Their basic English is limited, with few if any oral or writing skills. Parents then have difficulty in talking or listening to their child's teachers, helping with homework, or taking part in school events.
- They don't have information about registration, applying for special programs that might exist, school policies, calendars of events, scholarships, and resources.. Translation is sporadically offered, if at all, and most newsletters are only in English.
- When low-income parents with limited job or language skills work in low-paying jobs with long hours, their children are at risk of becoming latch-key kids, getting little if any help with homework, having flimsy working habits, and eating improperly. Boredom can create pressure to hook up with the wrong crowds.
- Bilingual teachers and aides are rare, and when they exist, they're generally overworked and can't give children the proper attention.

Results of cultural and language barriers:

- Continually rising number of high school drop-outs
- Involvement with gangs and gang violence
- Difficulty in mastering appropriate communication styles
- Misunderstandings — both cultural and linguistically

- Difficult adjustment to any new environment, both physical and emotional
- A widening gap between generations and peer groups
- Developing a sense of isolation due to few if any bilingual support personnel in school
- Latch-key kids and possible truancy can result in youth violence
- Danger of illness or even death from lack of health-related information or having enough to eat or proper medication

Frustrations mount for culturally diverse parents.

The irony is that schools and teachers want parents to take part in activities in the school, yet parents get little information, either about how the general education system or the school itself works, or what parents can do to participate. If a parent's cultural background doesn't provide this, the parent can't respond. The traditional ways that parents help in a school don't apply when parents can't grasp the basics. Parents who really suffer are those who are isolated by their language and/or their ethnic background. We need to start where the parent is, not expect them to join in where we are.

What about low-income, culturally diverse families?

When parents have little money, limited command of a language, and few skills for making a living, their focus is on pure survival. They seldom have time to consider an involvement in their child's education beyond the bare minimum. They isolate themselves from the school: it's too low on their survival priority list. The school and the teachers may well have tried to reach out to these parents but nothing works. Nothing *can* work, because surviving takes precedence.

In time, the school turns away in frustration, leaving the parent and sometimes the child behind. The result: parents — and students — who feel angry, envious, apathetic, hurt, isolated, and depressed. In time, their interests in school, in education, in learning, all dissipate. This lack of involvement begins to create a chain reaction: A barrier rises between the children and the teacher, another between the parents and the school. The expectations for the child on the part of parents sink even lower, and the impact on the child is ultimately a negative one—one that can last a lifetime.

What Makes an "Involved Parent?"

Involved parents are:
- **Active.** They accomplish things, participate in activities, organize and/or complete tasks, instigate change—at home, in the school, and in their community.
- **Supportive.** They encourage and support children, they understand, empathize, listen, communicate, and commit themselves to education.

Parents tend to fall into one of these four categories:

Category #1: This parent genuinely wants to learn and help. She is active in the PTA/PTO, goes to workshops, helps run a booth, writes grants, photocopies newsletters. This category has the fewest members, seldom more than 10 percent of parents.

Category #2: This parent cares deeply about his child's education, but is more comfortable working with his child at home and at his own pace. He reluctantly gets involved with some school-based activities, as long as there are a lot of other people there.

Category #3: This parent is all show and little go. She shows off her participation at school with lots of hullabaloo, but doesn't always follow through. At home, she's either indifferent or outright helpless. Her homework help is virtually non-existent.

Category #4: This parent's everyday life is so desperate that mere survival is the family goal. Working with his child

When parents are involved in the learning process, whole schools get better. When schools get better, children learn more. As children learn more, they value education more. As they value it more, they learn even more and pass it on to their own kids.
—Missouri Governor John Ashcroft

takes second place, if any at all. This category of parent needs the most help yet is the least responsive or able to contribute.

Involved parents nurture involved children

Research consistently states that when teachers involve parents, student achievement measurably improves. These children steadily progress in reading, they do more homework, and they have a more positive attitude toward school than children whose parents are not involved in many or any ways. Schools with a viable and vital parent-involvement program produce students who perform better than other schools with similar programs that either aren't doing as thorough a job of involving parents, or can't involve them at all.

Gallup polls reflect the attitudes of teachers: Teachers think that parent involvement is a significant variable for student success, and they want parents to be involved, or more active. Teachers and parents both agree that they need parent-involvement programs that are long-term, organized, reflect the student body fairly, are objectively planned, and that continue to strengthen the bonds between teachers and parents, students, and communities.

Involved parents provide a strong link for change.

When families teach and help their children, the teacher experiences tangible results. The child of an involved parent is more receptive to information conveyed in a school setting, is better adapted to work with other children, and creates fewer fights and more solutions than the child whose parents are not involved.

Teachers are grateful for these children — and for their parents. They send strong messages of approval to the children and their parents. The parents are then more receptive to the work of the teacher and the school, and reciprocate by showing their support. This cycle is a positive and stimulating one, and the vital link is parent involvement. When it's missing, a student must work much harder to reconcile learning habits at school with those at home.

Parent Enthusiasm Or Parent Burnout

What grade is your child in...?

Often, the old-timers in a PTA view the eager new parents with a jaundiced eye, knowing that the majority of them will sooner or later fall by the wayside, along with their original ideas, boundless energy, and varied views, which range from optimism to dissatisfaction. Researchers have looked at parent participation in different ways over the years, and their findings support what many parents and teachers have personally experienced:

- **Pre-Kindergarten through 2nd Grade:** These parents tend to be the most energetic, but the least effective. They're delighted that their child is finally in school. They want their child to succeed. They feel the enormity of a school and the school system, and many are in awe or even intimidated. They seek out other parents to connect with. Homework hasn't become much of an issue with children at this age, and parents' skills, or lack of them, aren't yet obvious. Homework isn't taking up much if any time in the evenings. The result is a parent who feels quite confident that she or he is a strong influence in the child's success.

- **3rd through 6th grades:** Parents in this group tend to drop out like flies. By now, many of these parents haven't been working very effectively with the teacher and aren't asking for or getting guidelines for home learning. These parents may feel that their skills in English, or in math, reading, history, science, or other subjects, are not strong enough for them to genuinely help their child. Other parents have gone back to work because they feel their child is independent now and doesn't need the parent as much, and the family needs the income.

- **Middle School:** Many parents of children in middle school lose motivation to help their child with homework or school assignments. They feel incapable of academically guiding their child, and peer pressure, along with their child's growing independence, can create emotional distance between parent and child. Unlike elementary school, middle school is a place where children regularly interact with several teachers each day.

- **High School:** Hormones, gender, and peer culture differences create an enormous barrier between most parents and children of this age. Students are now embarrassed rather than proud when their parents get involved in school activities, and the directions that students take are often quite different than the parent would like. A parent stays involved almost in spite of his or her child rather than because of the child. However, parents who involve themselves early on are more likely to have children who accept, even approve of, continuing involvement on the part of parents through high school.

How Parent Involvement Benefits Schools

It makes life a lot easier....

Strong partnerships between families and teachers build an electric atmosphere in the school, the classroom, the community, and the home. It can create trust and optimism, and an excitement for learning. An involved parent can remove some of the isolation a teacher can feel when fighting a lonely battle for the child's education. Ongoing involvement on the part of the parent can be seen as a form of burn-out prevention, allowing a teacher to dedicate more time and energy to teaching.

Teachers are the essential link

When teachers make a commitment to reach out to parents, encouraging and supporting their efforts, they create an expanding circle that surrounds the children and protects their interests. This commitment then brings parents into the circle and keeps all the players involved, and encouraged.

If the teacher doesn't initiate and follow through on parent-involvement activities, then only those parents who would participate anyway will be involved.
—Dr. Joyce Epstein

What's expected of the teacher in parent involvement?

For teachers to effectively reach out to parents and genuinely involve them, they must start by:

- Welcoming each and every family into the classroom and school.

- Establishing two-way communication and dialogue.

- Respecting each child and his or her family.
- Looking at their own possible prejudices toward the child's ability, background, culture, linguistic ability, appearance.
- Holding high expectations for each child to learn and grow.
- Understanding the community's history, customs, leaders, school history, values, and concerns and the place of the students and families in that community.

The teacher can involve those who have been historically uninvolved.

In most every group of parents, there are those faithful few who have always gotten involved, regardless of the circumstances. There are also the parents who can't or won't take any part. The teacher can play a crucial role in taking this latter group of uninvolved parents, and strategically turning them around. The more that these parents can take part, the more promising it is for their child, and for all the children in the classroom and the school. When the core group grows and expands to include parents from diverse and varied backgrounds, the students blossom. The circle widens and everyone inside it is a true partner.

What keeps so many parents away?

Most people who work with volunteer groups talk fondly of the "core group." In any given group of parents, for example, there are those few people who always run a booth, bake brownies, work the copy machine, or design flyers. They're always there, and they seldom burn out. When those parents reach out to other parents, they initially respond to pleas for help, but after one or two tries, they draw back. The goal? Find out why. Reach them before they disappear.

What happens when parents won't get involved?

Typically, a precious few in any group do the work of the many. Parents and parents' groups are no exception. On a national scale, for example, only about 2% of eligible voters even take the time to vote in their local school-board elections. We need to project how these realities impact on our nation, our schools, our children, our families and, importantly, on the future of our country and our world. When we look objectively at the facts as they are now, what is the impact of isolated children and uninvolved parents on our future?

What's a possible scenario of a country with under-educated children and stressed-out teachers?

- **Our country's problems will be compounded.** Unemployment will skyrocket due to unskilled and under-qualified young people.

- **Businesses will spend billions.** Potential employers will spend untold amounts in an attempt to train under-educated workers, ruling out salary increases, pensions, IRAs, and the creation of more jobs.

- **Youth violence.** Children will continue getting involved in gang activities in the country's streets, schools and homes.

- **Teenage pregnancies.** More babies will be having babies, and more of these children will be doomed to living in poverty with little eduction or encouragement to succeed. They will continue to chain of dependence on social services..

- **Homelessness.** More families and children will be left homeless, living on the streets in constant danger and in poor health.

- **Budget strain.** The American taxpayers will be footing the bill for these failures, at city, state, and national levels in an already over-stressed economy.

Administrators Play a Crucial Role

The role of an educational administrator is often limited by the overwhelming demands of the system. And, often, the administrator must limit himself or herself to just fulfilling the needs put forth by teachers, staff, students, and the running of a school. When an administrator can reach out to families and use the energy and skills of parents to augment his or her efforts, a new dimension of success can begin for that administrator.

What do the experts recommend?

The American Association of School Administrators (AASA) and the National School Boards Association (NSBA) jointly produced a report entitled "Beyond the Schools: How Schools & Communities Must Collaborate to Solve the Problems Facing America's Youth." They made four recommendations. Significantly, two of the four involve parents. The recommended strategies, and their rationale follow:

- **Involve parents and other adult volunteers.** Research has shown that parents' involvement is a prime determinant in children's learning and the success of schools. And today, when there are many parents who are not actively involved in their children's education, it's also important to recruit outside adult volunteers to help children and youth in need.

- **Offer a parent education program in every school.** When parents understand their roles and responsibilities, they are better able to help their children. Parents of children at risk might not know what to expect at various stages of child development. They might not understand the impact of the example they set as a child's first teacher and role model.

What role can an administrator take in supporting the involvement of families?

An administrator, principal, vice principal, or educator in a leadership role within the school deals often with parents. An administrator who is an effective leader is sensitive to parents' needs and vulnerabilities, and to the parents' real expectations for their child. There are many reasons a parent may feel reticent to get involved in the school, and it's the role of an administrator to understand and appreciate these sources. Parents can feel intimidated by a school that's quite unlike the one they attended as a child. They may have cultural or language barriers to hurdle. They can carry bad feelings with them from their own school experiences, or have no experience with a system that appears monolithic and impersonal.

The evolved administrator supports involved parents

The administrator who values parent involvement takes responsibility for ensuring that the teachers and staff in the school are trained to recognize and encourage the participation of parents. This administrator also works directly with parents and gives them avenues of approach to get closer to the teacher and staff. She or he regularly provides many kinds of options and opportunities for parents to have a voice in the decision-making process of the school; the administrator understands the value of community participation and invites community members to take an active role in the school.

The following is a valuable listing of goals that administrators can work toward reaching, together with the teachers and parents in their schools. The end result is a network of collaborative partnerships and effective parent-educator teams, with the student declared the ultimate winner.

TEN CRITICAL STEPS IN FORGING PARENT-SCHOOL CONNECTIONS

by Lillian Brinkley, President
The National Assoc. of Elementary School Principals

1. We must go to the families, not wait for them to come to the school.

2. We must make our schools family-friendly.

3. We must be sensitive to families' needs and to their cultural differences.

4. We must convince our school districts to make family involvement in education a priority and to adopt appropriate policies.

5. We must adapt school days and vacations to today's families' schedules.

6. We must forge partnerships with our communities, including providers of social services and child care.

7. We must provide information and guidance to help parents be good parents.

8. We must tell families what we're doing in school and why.

9. We must help our teachers develop strong home-school relationships.

10. We must make family involvement a critical part of teacher training.

The Major Components of an Effective Parent-Involvement Program

An effective Parent-involvement Program is one that works for and grows with all its players. It fosters mutual respect, caring, and a shared sense of purpose and equality. Its components are:

COMPONENT #1: Dialogue Between Home and School:
- This is the most vital component. It includes information exchange between the child, the parents, teachers and school. Each helps the other to assist the child in learning.
- The parents are contacted regularly through workable and recognized channels, such as email, newsletters, and/or phone calls. Communication works two ways: it's important that the school open channels that welcome parents' communications.
- Parents have hopes and dreams, concerns, vulnerabilities, areas of despair and of great expectations. Teachers and administrators benefit when these feelings are encouraged and communicated.

COMPONENT #2: Parents at Home:
- Parents take care of the basics: food and nutrition, shelter and warmth, clothing and other essential needs of the child. They also encourage learning by reading aloud, helping with homework and talking about children's interests and concerns.

COMPONENT #3: **Parents at School:**
- Parents show their support through activities that fall largely under the traditional umbrella, such as various kinds of fund raising, going on field trips, being an appreciative audience for student performances, chorus, and dance recitals, helping with events like the book fair, and taking part in the school's general well being.

COMPONENT #4: **Teacher Reaches Out to the Home**
- The teacher welcomes and motivates parents to take part in the classroom and gives them direction, options, and opportunities.
- The teacher informs the parents about school-wide activities, as well as providing some resources to assist actively in home learning.

COMPONENT #5: **School Reaches Out to the Home**
- The administrators and staff work closely with families, helping them with social services and agency referrals.
- The school works with parents and students, collecting items to help needy families with clothing, food — especially during holidays — and home visits for families that don't come into school.

COMPONENT #6: **Home-School Collaboration**
- Parents learn to work with teachers and staff by becoming familiar with the policies of the school, understanding more about the school curriculum, and by sharpening their communication and listening skills.
- Teachers and staff learn to work with families, improving their communication skills, focusing on their conferencing abilities, offering parents a wide variety of classroom activities to get involved in, creating homework that educates and stimulates the students and challenges the parent.

COMPONENT #7: Home-School Learning
- Parents — as the child's first and potentially best teachers — work closely with the teacher and the school to create and reinforce a stimulating model for optimum learning, both at home and at school. Under the teacher's guidance, parents might choose to work with the teacher in the classroom, tutoring one-on-one or in small groups. The teacher supervises, educates, and works closely with the parent prior to and during tutoring. Both teacher and parent then evaluate their progress.
- Teachers work closely with administrators, other staff members, and outside resources to look at exciting alternatives for teachers and parents to use together. The teacher can visit families at home, working with them on ways to help their child thrive.

COMPONENT #8: Home-School Advocate
- Parent volunteers work closely with teachers, administrators, and staff for ideas and pointers about how to be a strong advocate. Options and alternatives are brainstormed for ways to be heard by decision-makers, to further advocate for children, to problem-solve and to formulate strong viewpoints on policies and goals.

COMPONENT #9: A Home-School Council
- Consisting of parents, teachers, administrators, staff, and children (when age-appropriate) school-wide, and representing all grades, the Home-School Council creates a bridge between home and school. The Council's vision is reflected in its program, which provides opportunities for members to be mutually supportive, enthusiastic, positive, and forward-moving.
- The program consists, along with many other possibilities, of:
    —A mission and vision statement
    —Guidelines for its members, such as by-laws

—The results of parent surveys
—Names, addresses, children's names, and classes for a data base
—A range of activities that appeal to the various target groups of the Council
—A planning calendar that gives information on activities
—The school handbook
—An article or document that explains the big picture of the educational system that governs the school

—Information about the PTA or PTO

- The Home-School Council drafts and approves a direct-action plan that escalates the current state of events and brings it closer to the ultimate vision of the Council.
- The plan sets short-term and long-term goals in both the individual class and the entire school, such as creating an after-school program. Other reachable goals include:

  —Create or improve the school newsletter
  —Organize a volunteer home-visit program
  —Develop and distribute stimulating materials for home learning

Starting a Parent-Involvement Program in Ten Steps

The players, regions, backgrounds, and languages may differ, but the roots of parent-involvement program development are the same:

Step #1: What's Needed and Wanted

What are the goals in starting a program for involving parents? What are the problems that need solving? What do the *specific* parents, children and/or teachers of this *specific* group need in order to succeed? Design a comprehensive plan of action, and write it up. Bring together as many interested parents as possible to lend strength to the idea.

Step #2: Money, Money, Money

How much money is needed to make the plan of action succeed? What are the priorities? List various sources of possible revenue: fund raising, grants, donations, allocations, budget reassignments.

Step #3: Elect a Chairperson

What kind of person has the qualifications and connections to do this job well? Is he or she a parent, a community member or both? After being elected, he or she reviews the plan of action, looks at the goals and needs of the group, and recruits various people to serve on the committee.

Step #4: Strategize, Organize

There's a game plan, a funded budget, a leader and committee members. Now reality hits. As a group, look at the overall game plan. Does it need to be revamped or reviewed for options? Look at strategies that are specific to the needs and the people.

Step #5: Offer Incentives

Reach out to parents with offerings of raffle prizes, door prizes, special trips, workshops, seminars, pizza parties for the children. Help them access social services and assistance with problems.

Step #6: Build Relationships

The leader and the group — as individuals and as a committee — explore ways of opening new doors to parents, other community members, school staff, district personnel, decision-makers, local businesses. They act decisively to keep the doors open.

Step #7: Give Positive Feedback

Give parents and other team players a sense of their accomplishment and ownership. Make decisions as a group. Let the children share the pride of the parents' involvement. Keep attitudes respectful and positive toward all parents and each child.

Step #8: Expand and Grow

Chronicle your successes. Talk to other school, community, city, state, and federal programs. Explore collaborative potential. Write articles, make approaches to media. Spread the word!

Step #9: Keep It Going

Don't rest on your laurels. Continue to assess group goals and to see where you still need to go.

Step #10: Say Thank You

A successful parent-involvement program involves people who care. Make sure they know how valuable they are.

What Are the Obstacles to Parent Involvement?

The best of intentions often hit a brick wall.

You hold a parent's meeting — and one percent of the parent body shows up. You outfit a parents' resource room, and you're the only one who uses it. You plan a workshop. Three parents attend after 6 long weeks of organizing. What keeps the parents away ? The reality is that in any volunteer group, there are those who get involved, and those that can't or won't. The challenge is to first understand the latter group, their reservations and realities, and to use that understanding to help bring them into the group of parents who do get involved. That understanding can be a very powerful weapon.

The trouble with us is too much apathy. But who cares?
—Lucy to Charlie Brown

What keeps parents from getting involved?

- **Isolation.** Many schools — whether urban or rural — simply have a tradition of isolation. In many cases, the family lives too far from school either for home visits or for the parents to come to school — or they live in an area considered dangerous.

- **Discouragement.** Many parents honestly feel that their involvement makes no real or lasting difference in their child's education.

- **Weak links.** The schools and the community seldom reach out to one another; when they do, it's a feeble effort at best, despite the best of intentions.

- **School-based objections.** In many cases, teachers, staff, and even district-based administrators prefer keeping parents at arm's length or giving them minimal and low-level tasks.

- **Income and/or class barriers.** Low-income families have more difficulty realizing the benefits of parent involvement, and are less likely to have or keep strong connections with the school. Ironically, they often consider themselves easy to reach and will come when asked, but seldom come unbidden.

- **Intimidation.** Parents — especially those with disadvantaged children — see the school as a powerful and impersonal institution. This vision often conjures up negative associations with similar institutions in their own past. They may see the school as symbolic of society as a whole, one that's treated them badly. Personnel connected with this monolithic institution can be viewed with distrust and suspicion.

- **Diversity creates miscommunications.** In schools where there is a moderate-to-high ethnic population, there is often a lack of understanding between the school and the parents in areas of:
    - language
    - customs
    - communication styles
    - income and entitlement
    - education
    - religion
    - attitudes
    - expectations.

  In these schools, there is seldom any cultural sensitivity-training for teachers, staff, administrators — or parents.

- **Inept communication.** At those unavoidable times when the parent-teacher meetings aren't on time, or are poorly scheduled, or when notices aren't sent home with enough advance notice, parents can be confused or frustrated. Often parents have some difficulty finding time that's mutually convenient for parent-teacher meetings. And usually any direct teacher or school communication with the parent concerns a negative issue or problem.

- **Minimal parent-involvement training.** Because parent involvement is undervalued, the schools don't often encourage or offer staff development in this area. This also sends a message to the staff that parent involvement is an unimportant issue. This message begins in many teachers colleges where parents are often viewed as an interruption or diversion for the classroom.

- **No direction.** Some parents may genuinely want to help but they don't know where to turn or how to start. The school, teachers, and other parents may assume these parents are capable of finding their niche; in fact, they feel helpless, uncomfortable or awkward.

- **Schools bring up emotions.** Many parents, even well-educated and capable parents, often have very emotional reactions to their child's school. They may feel guilt or resentment, fear, envy, inadequacy, or be very shy. Being in school can bring back memories of childhood failure or abuse.

- **Teachers over-stressed and discouraged.** Most teachers are grappling with schedules already overcrowded, and are often underpaid. In many cases, teacher unions or organizations, or local and state school board rules circuitously discourage teachers' enthusiasm for working with parents.

- **Undervalued.** Sometimes parents who may have tried to offer their skills, time, or energy have not been called upon, or have been used badly. Teachers may also have pre-labeled parents, thinking of them as inept, under-qualified to help, poor speakers, limited, or lower-class.

- **Resistant teachers.** Teachers might be concerned that parents, once they are given any control, will interfere with classroom regulations or conduct. The teachers may harbor prejudices about families that are low-income, minority, or even parents who are privileged, seeing them as hard-to-reach, difficult, uninterested, or non-supportive, or feeling entitled to special privileges.

- **Parents can lack the basics.** Some parents may not have transportation to come to school meetings or events, or may need child care which they can't afford or find at those times. They might be insecure about their clothing or general appearance, either due to income or cultural differences.

- **Different expectations.** Parents and teachers may hold two different sets of expectations, and both feel frustrated when these expectations don't have a tangible pay-off.

- **Inadequate funding.** Many schools or groups simply cannot afford to offer parent-involvement training to staff or parents, or they can't direct them to the proper resources. The group has little real opportunity for raising funds, writing grants, or using other methods of raising money for training.

- **Communication barriers.** Often communication is one-way, going from school to home with little encouragement for two-way dialogue. Notices or flyers are generally offered only in English, even if other language(s) may be spoken by the parents. In many cases, the information sent home is written or graphically presented in ways that don't really inform or catch the eye.

- **Fear of discovery.** Sometimes parents are in this country illegally, are undocumented, or fear repercussion from the authorities. The school often represents the center of authority to many parents who avoid having anything to do with it.

- **Abusive home conditions.** Many families are struggling with simply surviving on a day-today basis. Domestic violence, drug and alcohol abuse, crime-infested neighborhoods, over-crowded homes, teen-age pregnancy, absence of one or both parents — all contribute to living in a basic survival mode.

Although the overall picture may appear dismal, the exact opposite is true...!

In order to be effective, one must first look at the existing realities. In accepting them, one can then counter-attack. For each of the above barriers, there is a strategy to hurdle the barrier. For each obstacle there is a solution.

Throughout *The Do's and Don'ts of Parent Involvement*, we examine the many methods of overcoming the harsh realities and reasons for parents' uninvolvement. In the process, we offer exciting and very doable options for reaching parents, successfully bringing families into a parent-involvement program, and creating a thriving atmosphere for all concerned.

Anything worth doing is worth fighting for. The end results can create children who are successful lifelong learners, and parents, educators, staff, and administrators who are directly responsible for creating positive conditions for the students. The rewards last a lifetime.

The Great Rewards of Parent Involvement

Massive teamwork — and individual efforts — working together.

In the face of obstacles and barriers to parent involvement the payoff is in the final benefits. When parents, community members, and educators work alongside one another, we can isolate and provide resources that can help our children now, as well as contribute to their future.

The rewards of parent involvement for families:

- **Pride in the child.** The primary goal of parent involvement is seeing that the child becomes a learner, grows, and evolves into a lifelong learner. When a parent sees this happen, pride of accomplishment is the supreme reward.

- **Learning specifics.** Parents often want to become more involved in their child's growth, and to become a better parent. They can do this more easily in a parent-involvement program with information, training, direction, and advice.

- **Lower domestic violence.** In families where there is strong parent involvement, violence goes down when understanding goes up. An informed parent can learn to seek agency assistance, and work with support groups.

- **Stronger sense of self.** Self-esteem, self-confidence, decision-making skills and leadership potential rise

Think of a child's imagination as wet cement, and each of our responses shapes his character.
—Dr. Haim Ginott

when a parent works to strengthen and improve his or her family.

- **Communications.** Skills of conversational style, listening, asking questions, and improving interpersonal relationships with children, teachers, and parents.

- **Delinquency falls.** The rates of juvenile delinquency fall dramatically when the child's parents take the time and energy to get involved.

- **Builds appreciation of others.** Once a parent is involved, he or she sees with a new clarity how teachers, administrators, other parents, the whole system of education and government work, and what each component's role is.

- **Increases personal motivation.** Involvement inspires self-growth, new interest, and stronger motivation to build one's own skills and education.

- **Expands networking.** Parents meet other parents who have business and personal connections and resources, like job referrals and day care options.

- **Access to resources.** Information on parenting, vocational skills, discipline, conflict resolution, health-related issues, all become more available.

The rewards of parent involvement for children:

- **Higher success in school.** Far fewer learning problems are family related. The child usually experiences a greater growth in academic progress. Social problems generally decrease when involvement increases. Attendance gets better and steadier, behavior problems decline.

- **More motivation to succeed.** A stronger sense of possibility for the future and a more developed sense of self to accomplish dreams. Decision-making skills and leadership abilities rise to the surface.

- **Less substance abuse.** Drug, alcohol, and tobacco abuse are lessened for the child, during school and in the years after school.

- **Greater understanding.** When the parents get involved, the child has a stronger sense of the "big picture," by seeing it differently and through the eyes of the parents. Attitudes markedly improve. Communication gets better and more frequent between the child and his or her teacher, parent, and other children.

- **Healthy growth.** When a child's parents get involved in his or her life, it generally imbues the child with a sense of pride and accomplishment, increasing his or her self-concept and self-esteem. An involved parent can usually provide more help for his or her child, understand the mission of the school and the task of the teacher.

- **Peer pressure decrease.** When parents get more involved, the child frequently gets more needed attention, lessening the need for approval from outside sources. A child can turn in trust to a parent or guiding adult, rather than to peers with possible negative influences.

- **Attitudes improve.** With the insight and growth that comes when parents get involved, a child's viewpoints and attitudes may improve in a number of areas, including homework, school, family life, and relationships.

The rewards of parent involvement for educators:

- **Teacher satisfaction.** The overall effectiveness of teachers' work increases when parents get involved. The teacher feels the spirit of supportive parents who have a direct stake in seeing the teacher succeed. When an effective parent works well with the teacher in creating a dynamic collaboration, it works for the students, it gives the teacher more time for teaching, and the parent feels a sense of accomplishment.

- **Parent empathy.** When a parent works closely with a teacher for a while, the parent begins to see and understand how challenging teaching can be, and how well teachers meet their many challenges. Usually, the parent feels a stronger commitment to work with the teacher; consequently, interpersonal skills improve for both parties, and communication lines open up.

- **Parent learning.** A teacher is almost always the sole source of homework tips and guidelines for the parent. When parents and teachers collaborate through home learning, parents tend to think more highly of the teacher's abilities and skills. An effective teacher encourages the parents to create or enhance other ways to work with their child.

- **Job satisfaction.** Teachers who enjoy a moderate to high level of parent involvement in their classrooms feel much more positive about their jobs, and tend to stay in the teaching profession considerably longer than their less satisfied counterparts.

- **Better morale.** When a teacher is getting through to both the student and the parent, he or she has a higher feeling of self-esteem, self-concept, and morale. He or she feels a stronger commitment to the future of teaching and learning, and approaches the day-to-day aspects of teaching with enthusiasm.

- **Efficiency.** A teacher must divide his or her time between many students every day. Ideally, a parent at home spends concentrated time with just one student which makes the teacher's work more efficient.

- **Community backup.** When individual community members, who are also parents, begin to have an understanding of the teacher's role, they all stand more firmly and solidly behind the teacher and the school.

The rewards of parent involvement for the community:

- **Skills building.** When all members of a community work together, they share skills, collaborate on planning, and organize and complete projects. This works on both a collective and an individual basis.

- **Problem solving.** Resources, leaders and planners work together with schools and parents to isolate and solve community-based problems.

- **More resources.** When community and schools pool their facilities and materials, there is more chance of collaboration and mutual usages.

- **Cost effectiveness.** When services and facilities are pooled in a collaborative venture, money that would ordinarily go to each of them is re-directed to a single purpose.

- **Community pride.** Accomplishment builds self-esteem and pride, and that pride, in turn, spreads over all the constituents.

- **Global democratization.** The ripple effect of parents who are involved and growing along with their children and their children's educators ultimately reaches into many nooks and crannies of our national system of education.

The Essential Elements of Parent Involvement

Where do we go from here?

We've explored the need for parent involvement, and we've seen the obstacles that impede effective involvement. We've looked at the rich, great rewards of parent involvement.

In Section Two, we'll examine the myriad strategies and directions for getting parents involved, but before we do, we need to be crystal clear about what the essential elements of a successful parent-involvement program really are:

- **Start where the parent is at.** Reach out to the parent. Find out where the parent really is, not where you wish he or she were. Match a task or a strategy of involvement with a parent's own need and ability.

- **Be creative.** Find and create ways of reaching parents that are unique, fun, creative, and responsive to the need and ability of the parent. Design materials that reach out to people and cause them to reach back. Personalize communications that are sent home.

- **Communicate.** Replace bad communication habits with new skills. Learn to listen to the people around you, really listen. Find ways of controlling anger. Understand cultural diversity and how that impacts on communication styles, use of language, and non-verbal body language. Translate notices and letters into other languages, and provide translators at meetings.

- **Keep expectations reasonable.** Don't expect too much, too soon. This only dissipates needed energies. A parent-involvement program is composed of dozens of baby steps rather than a few giant leaps. Tell people what your expectations of them are, and ask for the same back from them.

- **Set goals together.** When the group makes a plan of action and sets goals together, the entire group feels collaborative and involved in seeing that the final goals are met. The rules, guidelines, regulations, suggested options — all are part of this group decision-making process.

- **Mutual trust.** In a group dynamic, it's vital that the members trust one another and have confidence in each other's abilities and skills; that they can confide in each other, and have an ultimate faith in their ability to pull together as a group supporting any idea.

- **Parent liaison.** Find a parent advocate with a strong desire to work directly with parents in meeting their own needs. This is especially valuable for parents of an at-risk or special-needs child.

- **Offer options.** Look at the needs and capabilities of the parents in the group and go from there. Offer ways a parent can come into the group on various levels, from low-risk, low-level tasks (like child care and refreshments) to high-profile opportunities (like grant writing or running for school board).

- **Meet people personally.** Get a strong sense of who the parents really are as human beings, rather than being known only as "Justin's mom," or as the man "who lives in the projects," or as "one of the Hispanic mothers." The more we know about each other's cultures, habits, protocols, and communication styles, the better we can fill mutual needs. Make parents feel welcomed and included by offering child care, food, and comfortable chairs.

People need to feel they belong to a group. They want to feel that the group needs them in order to reach mutual goals, and that they are appreciated.

- **Positive challenge.** People in a group want and need to feel challenged and utilized, rather than ignored, misused, or abused. Give people a chance to show off their peak performances whenever possible. Make them feel like stars!

- **Reach goals.** People in a group who have worked together, and as individuals, to make something happen need to feel that they are making some kind of progress, and that they're getting closer to their goals. They thrive on seeing that what they're doing is worth all the effort. This occurs through validation when the goal is reached, as well as by using incentives and rewards, and by keeping close touch with the project and the people working on it.

Section Two
Reaching Out!

Section Two represents the heart beat of this book. It's a compilation of wisdom that I've gleaned from parents, educators, community leaders and other sources along the way. You'll find hands-on projects and ideas with options; also event possibilities, reproducible sample pages, quick tips, communication expanders, guidelines for conferences and organizing groups. The ideas in this collection have proven exceedingly successful for those who've shared them.

I've used these strategies myself; they've been a boon to my own work over the past years as PTA President, Co-President and Vice President in our Manhattan public school and serving on several district and city committees. Quite a few of these methods of involving parents have been invented on the spur of the moment and out of sheer necessity. Others are tried-and-true, sure-fire ways, used by people who are highly successful in the field of parent involvement.

Most of these strategies, however, are hard to come by. They're not easily accessible to the majority of people and groups looking to involve parents more thoroughly in an effective program. Guidebooks, textbooks, or even pamphlets are rare, and most are out-of-date. Few take into consideration the drastic changes taking place in today's explosive times. So reach out — absorb the strategies that apply to your own needs, and try them out on the parents who can potentially augment your own dreams, and add to the quality of the education you want to give their child. It'll take a little time, and you'll be frustrated more than once. But get out there. Give it a try...

Trying to educate children without the involvement of their family is like trying to play a basketball game without all the players on the court.
—Senator Bill Bradley

1. Reaching Out to Parents:
Take A Creative Approach

Parents usually feel complimented when people take the time to include them. And when the methods of inclusion are creative, respectful, informative, and fun, parents are much more likely to respond positively.

There are myriad ways of reaching out. Some of the ways include:

- **Survey the parents.** Find out what they want and need, as well as what their child needs. Surveys can also be sent to teachers, staff, and administrators to coordinate their needs with those of the parents.

- **Conduct informal parent meetings.** Select themes such as:

    —**Introductions** — to the school, staff, and teachers; school and discipline policies; curriculum choices; city and state school boards; and to local community groups.

    —**Brainstorming** — from fund raising to family workshops, ESL or parenting workshops, a school handbook, family science and math nights.

- **Interview parents.** Learn more about parents on a personal level. Talk about their academic and emotional concerns and expectations for their child. Interviews can take place in the home, school, or at another location.

The most interesting people were probably nerds in school. We have to encourage the differentness that children have, we have to permit and nurture uniqueness.
—Duane Michaels

- **Conduct home visits.** For parents who are reluctant to attend parent-teacher conferences, or who are home bound, have language barriers, or refuse to work with the school in any other way, a scheduled visit to the home can be an effective icebreaker.

- **Send positive messages home.** Teachers, administrators, and counselors can make phone calls to the family on a regular basis. They can also send notes home. The calls and notes give parents only positive messages about their child.

- **Provide newsletters.** Published by students, parents, teachers and community members, newsletters circulate information that represents everyone. Make them well-written, neat, informative, and fun.

- **Create special interest support groups.** Find out who needs representation in your school: single parent groups, gay and lesbian parents, grandparents as parents, step-parents, mothers, fathers, even siblings.

- **Hold workshops.** These can be facilitated by parents or by professionals, and can focus on topics like conflict resolution, parenting skills, discipline, AIDS, drug abuse, peer pressure, health, nutrition — or any other topic relevant to the parent body.

- **Use Media.** Set up an online or telephone hotline for parenting advice and problems, and organize a volunteer core to handle it. Talk to local public access TV channels to set up a TV hotline. Suggest that local talk shows feature more subjects like parenting, homework, and reading to your child.

- **Schedule social gatherings.** Events and informal gatherings are excellent social icebreakers where parents and teachers can meet. Food is the best icebreaker.

- **Create parent report cards.** They allow parents an opportunity to give their honest appraisal and evaluation of their observations of the school. They provide valuable information for the teacher and school as a whole.

- **Provide 24-hour recorded messages.** Rather than tying up a school line, the message can help with phone referrals, or announcing events and dates at the school.

- **Use references and electronic resources.** Dial-a-Teacher or a specific tie-in to a local library, information system, or an electronic encyclopedia that helps with homework or gathering information.

- **Send home a picture.** Get a clear photo of yourself. Photocopy it, and it becomes a logo for your own personalized stationery on which you send a note home to all parents of your new students. Ask them to send a picture back — their child, family, pets, along with information on the child that the parent and student would like the teacher to know. This practice helps the teacher match faces in the new school year, and it creates a nice bridge from the beginning.

- **Keep a Communications Strategy file.** Whenever you read an article or come across information that's pertinent to teaching or to parenting, clip it and keep it in a resource folder or binder. It reinforces your strategies and directions. It also serves to reassure any parents who need more resources that you're doing it right.

- **Welcome Parents to Your School.** At the beginning of each new school year, give each parent a "Welcome In" packet; if other languages are spoken in the school, translate as much of the information as possible. The packet can include:

    —A calendar of school events, test days, holidays, breaks

- —Advice on helping your child with math and science homework, reading to your child with age-appropriate book lists
- —A school or district handbook
- —A list of all teachers, support staff, aides and administrators, and a description of their roles in the school
- —The school discipline code
- —Classroom teachers' individual philosophy, rules, etc.
- —Information and events for the year from the Parent Association
- —A letter from the Principal on school history and philosophy
- —Medical information and school requirements
- —Recommended after-school programs and activities, in school or outside

• **Hone your communication skills.** Monitor yourself when you talk with parents. Are you making eye contact? Are you really listening, trying to hear and understand? Are you working hard at making yourself understood? Are you working as hard to understand them? Do you have a genuine caring for this person's child?

Include Culturally Diverse Parents and Students

Look at the possible outcomes of diversity issues.

Organize workshops and seminars that teach people the skills and tools that are designed to combat prejudice, and that teach increased sensitivity to the issues of culture, language barriers, diversity, customs, and sexual orientation. The key to effective communication is understanding the issues.

Look for ways to sponsor mentoring programs.

In many communities, individuals who have succeeded in business or in mastering a language, skill or craft, even in gaining a higher education, can pass along the advantages of their abilities by serving as a mentor to a parent who needs an extra hand and opportunity to advance him or herself.

Look honestly at the differences.

Only when people have a clear idea of the attitudinal and cultural differences that exist between them, and when they have been given information about these differences, can they then apply creative and positive problem-solving methods to clearing up the difficulties or problems that often arise from these differences.

Look at the numbers.

Get a demographic breakdown of the school's population from the principal's office or the local district school board.

When you look clearly at the numbers, you have a much better idea of who your population really is, and how you can target and reach each specific group.

Look at culture in the midst of communication.

Communication problems that arise among people are usually caused by a cultural influence on that communication. Some cultures think and speak in a direct and forceful way; others find directness to be offensive and tend to speak in vague metaphors or interwoven thoughts. Yet both cultures might reach the same conclusion in their own way.

Look for ways to reward.

Create a newsletter specifically for culturally diverse parents and students. Recognize their achievements and accomplishments and honor them by name. Have special events, like field trips, dances, musical performances, plays in their languages and honoring cultural events and aspects. Above all, keep in mind that each and every person deserves your respect.

Counselors Can Reach Out to Parents

Counselors promote emotional growth and unity

Virtually all school systems have either an in-house counselor or have access to one. The counselor often works with both the student and his or her family, as well as with the student's teacher, to promote positive social, emotional and academic growth.

Occasionally, the role of the counselor is underemphasized or misunderstood. Parents whose child or family could benefit from counseling aren't made aware of the role or the availability of the counselor. Some parents or students are ashamed or intimidated by their own problems, or by problems in the family. They might think no one can really help them. Their past experiences with the system have convinced them there's no hope. The following ideas will help you overcome these and other barriers:

- **Create a simple letter.** The counselor designs a simple note to send home to parents and students. Describe the multi-layered roles of a counselor and the counselors credentials and skills. Talk about who is eligible for the counselor's services, and the ways in which a counselor can help a student, a family and a teacher. Give clear instructions about how a student or family gets help. Assure privacy and a safe environment.

- **Conduct parent workshops.** The counselor can hold workshops for parents in improving their communication with their child in areas such as:
    - —Building self-esteem in the child
    - —Leadership skills
    - —Conflict-resolution in the family and the school
    - —Decision-making
    - —Helping a child avoid peer-pressure and gang influences and activities
    - —Child protection
    - _Bully Prevention
    - —Substance abuse prevention
- **Send home useful information for family development.** Make copies of articles and other information sources which can help parents and children grow closer together. Send them home with the child. Ask the child to share them with her family.

To: All Students and Parents of PS 41
From: Ms. Clayton, School Counselor

WHO IS A COUNSELOR?

A counselor is someone who listens and doesn't judge how you speak, or what you say, or what you're feeling. A counselor tells the truth, and keeps a secret.

A counselor is special because he or she listens when you're feeling lonely, sad, or mad. When something worries you so much that you can't really talk about it to anyone. When you're frightened, confused, down, or put-down. When school doesn't seem to be working out, or you're getting in fights.

I am a counselor. I'm here for each student, and I'm here for your family, too. If you ever need me, all you have to do is let me know. Leave me a note in the principal's office, or tell your teacher you'd like to see me. We'll talk a little bit, or maybe just take a walk together, and see what happens. That's about all. Easy.

My name is Ms. Clayton, and you can call me at 555-1234, email me at clayton@abc.com, or you can leave me a note in my mailbox in the school office. I'd like to get to know you better.

Note: You can add such elements as your credentials, years of service, days or hours available each week at school, etc.

Administrators Can Reach Out to Parents

- **Create a warm and welcoming environment.** Set the tone of the school with warm lighting, stimulating colors, changing exhibits. Decorate the hallways with students' artwork and writing projects. Keep the noise levels down when possible. Instill school pride in the children, staff, and parents.

- **Personally invite the parents to meet with you.** Send a note or warm letter home to the parents, welcoming them to the new school year. Outline your general plan for the year. Give parents the option of meeting with you, whether during a principal-parent breakfast, picnic, or afternoon tea. Create events around food that bring people together.

- **Pool the parent talent.** By taking a parent survey, find out some specific talents that the parents can offer the school. Match their skills and talents up with teachers, school personnel, or parent groups. This volunteer program can also involve the community.

- **Create a "Parents-only Program."** Parents often need extra help in areas like vocational training, ESL, or GED classes. Other parents can benefit from workshops and seminars in topics like parenting skills, discipline, homework help, health issues, preventing bully behavior, sex education, and communication skills.

No academic progress is possible...until there is a positive environment at the school where teachers, students, and parents like each other and work together for the good of all the students.
—James Comer

- **Consider starting a home-school council.** This council makes decisions that concern the school's curriculum, budgets, teacher hiring, and other issues that require thoughtful consideration. Teachers, parents, the principal and student representatives all form the school council.

- **Communicate with the parents monthly.** On a regular basis that the parents and students can count on, send home or email a newsletter that talks to the students, the parents, and the teachers, and preferably is contributed to by all three contingents. Send home a calendar that outlines various events—school-wide and by classroom. List school holidays, half-days, and parent-teacher conferences. When possible, coordinate the calendar with the PTA or parents' group, and cover their activities, too.

The Community Can Reach Out to Parents

The community brings parents together.

The impact of positive community-parent relationships can be profoundly effective in bringing about new levels of mutual understanding. The community has unique ways of reaching parents that schools don't have.

Some of the advantages that community groups and organizations can bring to parents are:

- **Encouragement.** A community group can encourage, help, and support parents, letting them know that their children are good people, with bright futures, and showing them that the family is an essential support system behind the child.

- **Environment.** A community group can provide strong models that show parents ways of creating a stimulating and positive home atmosphere for their child. It can model ways of reinforcing positive communication, mutual respect, guidelines, tools, and skills for effective parenting.

- **Enlightenment.** A community group can share its expectations, hopes, and dreams with parents concerning their children's future, and gives parents information that helps them understand the value of schools and how the school system operates.

- **Expectations.** A community group can gather information for parents about their child's school and the expectations the parents have for that school

There are only two lasting bequests we can hope to give our children. One of the is roots, the other, wings.
—Hodding Carter

in terms of academic growth, social behaviors, emotional well-being, physical health, and cultural exposure. It can help bring these expectations into perspective for the parents.

- **Exploration.** A community group can work closely with parents in developing unique and exciting approaches that stimulate the parents and reassure them that they can work — and grow — successfully with their child.

- **Enrichment.** A community group can look at ways for parents to enrich the standards of their own lives, financially, educationally, culturally, emotionally, and through career alternatives or adult education counseling.

- **Enlistment.** A community group can talk with other community agencies, creating strong collaborative networks. It can supply services and their coordination. It can reach out to parents and community, working together to raise the standards of education for the children of that community.

A liaison bridges community and parents

Personal outreach is the most effective way of reaching parents, bringing them in and keeping them involved. Studies show conclusively that approaching a parent, one-to-one, is the most likely way to engage that parent. But who is the contact person who represents the group? Within an effective community, a parent coordinator or community outreach person is someone who's qualified to make these connections. As a vital member of a parent involvement team, this community liaison is a valuable, integral component.

What does a community liaison need to do, or be?

A community liaison is an important link, bringing together many factions and issues. She or he needs a large share of diplomacy, must listen more than talks, and should respect fellow beings who all want the best out of life.

A successful community liaison:
- Starts where the parent is at, rather than following his or her own expectations of where the parent "should" be.
- Looks at life positively.
- Has a high energy level.
- Is respected in the community.
- Is known by the community and has family or business ties.
- Has excellent communication skills.
- Understands the cultural backgrounds of the community members.
- Believes in the school and its educational standards.
- Has a commitment to the concept of parent involvement and has strong organizational abilities to coordinate.
- Believes that the community and school are a good team and can continue to improve.
- Brings information from, and to, each of the team members.

The Business Community Can Reach Out to Parents

It's not just altruism...

Business communities are taking a hard look at their present and future work force and many are worried. More students are getting less from their education. More students are less skilled, less verbal, less equipped to make decisions, less likely to be leaders, or to have a global viewpoint. It benefits the business community to actively explore avenues of change. Students who continue to come into the world of business ill-prepared will seldom find employment, and business communities will have no workforce.

Parents are employees, and employers

The work force employs, and is employed by, people who are also parents. When these people all work together to encourage parent involvement in the education of their own children, and of the community's children as well, the future of a local and national workforce looks more substantial.

How can the business community promote parent involvement?

The possible directions are myriad, and with some creativity and a little extra time, a business can support and encourage parent involvement by:

- Working with schedules of employee parents to give them time to go to school-related meetings and conferences.

- When possible, awarding matching funds to encourage employees to donate money to their schools.
- Donating services, gift certificates, cash, or other viable goods to school fund raisers, like fairs, auctions, raffles, etc.
- Offering to provide tours of businesses to local school groups.
- Buying advertising space in school newspapers.

2. Keeping Parents Involved
You Have the Attention of Parents. Now What?

This is the crucial time. Your flyers have worked, the telephone tree or internet has connected parents with each other, and attendance at the last PTA meeting was close to ideal. But one meeting does not a membership make. You have to continue making these contacts, and keep on involving parents. You can reach them by using new and innovative approaches, and you can continue to use more traditional methods, too. Every parent can be reached, somehow.

The methods of reaching parents are unlimited

Every school and group has its own identity and styles of working together. But even within these confines, there are few boundaries around ways of reaching out to parents and families. The limits? Time and money, of course, are always in short supply. Add imagination and energy, and the horizons expand.

Understand the obstacles to parent involvement

Many parents feel at a loss to successfully help their children with homework, in the classroom, or with other issues at school. Some of the reasons are that parents:

- Feel it's strictly the school's job.
- Aren't proficient in English.
- Are intimidated by the school system and don't understand how it works.

"No," I say, "you are doing it wrong. You are failing as parents. You should be so vigorous, healthy, in the pink of condition (cut out all the smoking and drinking and coffee breaks), so inexhaustible, rambunctious, jolly, full of deviltry and frolic, of stories, of tomfoolery, of hilarity, that your children at last, after hours of violent exercise, worn down by laughter and intellectual excitement, with pale, neurasthenic frowns on their foreheads, cry: "Plee...ease, Mama, go to bed."
—Brenda Ueland

- Feel that teachers and administrators discourage parent participation.
- Have a cultural or language barrier.
- Had prior experiences with parent involvement that were mismanaged or negative.
- Want to help out but don't know how to start or whom to call.
- Prefer to keep their involvement contained inside the home, working one-on-one with their child.

Some Quick Tips

Teachers — and involved parents — can help by:

- Sending home suggested activities for parents to do with kids at home.
- Sending home tips about helping out with homework.
- Bringing parents into the current curriculum and study plan.
- Promoting parent and family workshops in:
    - —Learning English
    - —Family math
    - —Curriculum plans
    - —Vocational counseling and training
    - —Communication skills
    - —Parenting tips
    - —GED classes

Create a welcoming, friendly school environment

A first impression is one that lasts — positive or negative. Just a bit of extra time and energy can truly transform an environment and make it a welcoming one.

- Put a welcome sign on the front door — in all spoken languages.
- Work with the staff in genuinely welcoming parents and visitors.

- Establish a monthly time when parents of children in particular grades can meet with the principal or teacher, like a breakfast meeting before work and school starts. Provide childcare.
- Have parent and grandparent luncheons or dinners.
- Regularly send home school and classroom calendars that give dates of events, tests, field trips, up-dates.
- Decorate classrooms, hallways, cafeterias and school exteriors, and change decorations, with art work, paintings, collages.
- Paint hallways and classrooms with bright airy colors.

Support your PTA or parent group

Every school benefits from an active parent/teacher association or parent group. If not, it's the principal's responsibility to organize one by calling a parent meeting. With an established PTA or parents' group, all staff and administrators consult with the members when making policy, and work together on school-wide issues. Teachers should be encouraged to support and join in PTA or PTO events.

Respect the rights of parents

Parents' rights are now mandated by federal, state, city, and local boards. People working with parents benefit when they educate themselves about these rights, which include being allowed to examine their child's school records, learning about the roles of staff members, and knowing more about suspension conditions, discipline codes, and promotion policies.

Tell parents about your expectations for their children

One of the endearing ways of making partners out of parents is to let them know just what academic and behavioral expectations you have for their child. By making them clearer, parents can help to reinforce these expectations at home.

Bring parents into the classroom

Parents can be a vital and stimulating resource in the classroom. They can give new insights into cultural diversity, and can be positive role models. Some brief ideas are:

- Storytelling
- Reading aloud one-on-one
- Tutoring in math, reading, etc.
- Vocational training
- Speaking about specific topics of interest to the curriculum

Give parents some positive messages

Parents could easily feel that the only time they hear from the school is when there's trouble, which can understandably put both teachers and parents on the defensive. When parents are contacted by phone, email, or through a brief note home with positive comments about their child's test scores, attitudes, growth, or specific ways in which the child has participated, the results are long-lasting. And the parent feels more trust toward the teacher as well.

Involve parents in decision-making processes

Parents are taking an increasingly more direct role in the decision-making processes of their school. Now mandated in a widening circle of bases, parent involvement is crucial. Staff members can benefit by gaining more parent sensitivity to barriers: linguistic, cultural, racial, economic.

School-Based Management

In New York City, for example, one former chancellor instituted two initiatives to provide collaboration between parents and educators. One was called School-Based

Management/Shared Decision-Making (SBM/SDM), and the other was the Parent Involvement Program (PIP).

Under SBM/SDM, representatives of the whole school community — teachers, principal, parents, and upper-grade students — made management decisions. Over 200 public schools participated, with training, technical assistance, and support provided by the central district to parents on the team, ensuring that they were working effectively. The Board of Education assigned a facilitator, and the Office of Parent Involvement provided additional support for parent participants. Parents were trained to facilitate workshops for other parents in the areas of collaborative teamwork and communication skills, and school staff were given workshops geared toward breaking down the barriers between home and school.

Home-School Council

The focus of the home-school council is on the needs of children. The council is made up of delegates from a PTA or other parent group, as well as an equal number of teachers, student representatives, and the principal. The home-school council holds meetings on a regular basis that are open to the public, although only the elected members have voting privileges. Using a democratic process, the council reviews and makes decisions regarding topics like discipline codes, school rules, spending funds raised by the school, and a wide variety of issues.

Let parents know where they can get help

Parents often need more help than non-parents, whether economically, emotionally, or educationally. Too often, they don't get what they need because:

- They're ashamed to ask for help, especially in the area of parenting.
- They often think they should know everything automatically, and feel guilty when they don't.
- They don't understand the school, or the individual roles of the teachers, support staff, aides, administrators, community, or school district boards.
- They have no idea how to go about finding the proper resource.

- They have no liaison between the parents and the staff members to speak with.
- They have no staff member as ombudsperson for parents.

Include diverse members of the parent community

Different segments of the parent community, and their diverse cultures, habits, and languages make it imperative that people working with this community be sensitive and aware. Some special outreach issues are:

- Parents for whom English is a second language.
- Parents of children getting special education services.
- Families living in temporary housing.
- Families living in low-income housing.
- Families living in high-risk situations, such as domestic abuse, drug problems, gang violence, and extreme poverty..

Welcome all parents as partners in education

Encourage all parents to actively participate together in school activities. Some of the ways to enlist them are:

- Send out volunteer surveys — in appropriate languages — asking for donations of parent skills, time, advice, goods, and money.
- Put people to work when they volunteer. If you can't use them right away, make sure you tell them how much you appreciate their time.
- Target school-wide events to cover diverse populations, such as:
    - **Performances:** Music, songs, and dance performances by different cultures in costumes and in the language of the performers.

—**Food**: Sponsor an International Food Festival, with everyone contributing a cooked dish from the parent's culture.

—**Language courses:** Sponsor ESL classes, as well as classes in the other languages spoken in the school.

A word about translators

Make sure that notices are translated and that translators are available at all meetings. This can be a challenge in a school where several languages are spoken at home, but the communication it provides is vital to non-English speaking parents.

Keep your own interest level high

You've managed to get a lot of people interested, you've kept them involved and productive. Now you want to keep them feeling good — but you need to feel good, too. Genuinely good. And interested.

Try these basic strategies

Incorporate these practices in your own personal approach to parent involvement:

- Get to know parents as individuals. Be friendly, establish trust.
- When approaching parents about their child, always have something positive to say about the child — something you really believe is true.
- Offer activities based on what parents want or need.
- Be sensitive to customs, values, club, or church meeting times
- Always ask for and accept feedback from all key players

- Take pictures of children and/or parents working together, and display on a bulletin board (always ask permission first)
- Show your appreciation by:
    - —Display charts
    - —Scrapbooks
    - —Special tags and ribbons of accomplishment
    - —Thank you notes
    - —Formally acknowledging volunteers and special efforts at pre-announced events.

The student's environment is important, too

A teacher who wants a deeper understanding of his students explores the child's world outside the classroom. This world consists of home life, religious and cultural interests, personal interests, and hobbies.

The student who has captured her teacher's interest feels proud of herself, validated, respected, and tries harder to succeed.

There are ways to reach out to this student and the family environment that she comes from:

- **Send home a parent survey.** Ask that the survey be filled out by the parent and child together. Ask questions of the parents about their child's likes and dislikes, hobbies, career goals, special talents, pets, etc. Ask the parent to evaluate his child's strengths and areas that can be improved. Ask the parent questions about her own life, careers, dreams. When all the surveys have been brought back to you, go through them carefully and look for similarities, patterns, gaps, and ideas.
- **Look at areas of interest.** From the compiled surveys, list areas of interest. For example, if several of the students show a keen interest in fossils, bring in books, articles, videos, and magazines about fossils that these children can share with each other.

Their involvement often kindles the interests of other kids in the class, and whole class projects can emerge.

- **Invite parents to share their interests.** Look through the parent surveys, and find parents who have interests they can share with the class. These interests can tie directly into projects already in progress, or they can stand alone. The parent can talk to the class, show pictures or videos, take the class on a field trip, or conduct a tour through her business or area of interest.

- **Autobiographical projects.** Ask the students to:
    —Keep a daily journal about their lives.
    —Draw a map of their neighborhood.
    —Draw a picture of a favorite part of their home.
    —Write a poem or story about a typical day in their household.
    —Read the poem or story aloud to the class and to their family.

3. Gathering Information
Surveys

Why surveys...? How important *are* they?

We all get surveys in the mail — online, or in our favorite magazines. But they do fill an important function: Surveys help others find out who we are, what we want to have, and where we want to be.

Surveys sent home to parents, as well as to children, educators, and members of our community, bring back important information to the people whom we want to reach.

When should surveys be sent out to parents?

- At the first of the school year, to find out parents' skills, talents, willingness to volunteer for parent groups, and classroom needs.

- For parents new to the school, when school begins — to get their initial reactions —, and at the end of the year — to compare.

- After all parent-teacher conferences, to get suggestions concerning ways of improving them in the future.

- During mid-term breaks, to get a quick measure of what people think in the middle of the school year.

- At the end of the school year, to collect data on specific programs, school events, philosophies, specific incidents, and school personnel.

How are surveys distributed?
- Via kid mail — backpacks and pockets. This method may need extra incentives to reward the children for successful delivery.

- Distributed by hand at school events, outside school before and after hours, and at PTA meetings.

- Enclosed in the "Welcome to School" or registration packets.

- Mailed to each child's home. This runs into money but it's the surest way of guaranteeing the safe passage of the survey.

- Email to all parents who opt to be part of a class, or school-wide email list for daily homework assignments, or for school or class newsletters and announcements.

Hello Parents. We'd like to get to know you better...!!

Name _____ Phone _____

Address _____ Email _____

Children in Our School: Name _____ Age _____ Class _____

As a parent, I'd like to learn more about:
___ Ways I can help my child with homework.
___ How I can help the teacher in the classroom or help with school activities.
___ Ways I can help my children work out problems.
___ How to help my children get good food and health care.
___ Ways I can feel more comfortable talking with teachers.
___ How to understand more about the different cultures of people in our school.
___ Ways I can talk to my children about:
     ___ Sex education   ___ Drugs   ___ AIDS or Illness   ___Bullying
     ___ Death   ___ Values   ___ Handling Money   ___ Prejudice
___ How I can help my child with discipline and managing everyday conflicts.
___ Other topics, like:_____

I'd be interested in getting together with other parents and:
___ Getting to know them better.
___ Learning more about school management and related issues.
___ Finding out about community issues, such as:
     ___ School Board Elections ___ Community Leaders ___ Community Centers
___ Other topics, like:_____

I can attend meetings:
___ in the morning   ___ in the afternoon   ___ in the evenings   ___ on weekends

I'd prefer to meet:
___ in someone's home ___ at school ___ in the library ___ at the community center
Other suggestions are:_____

The meeting would be more enjoyable if there were:
___ Free child care   ___ Handicap access   ___ Refreshments
___Translation into _____ ___ Transportation from _____ to_____

The best way to contact me is:
___ Phone   ___ Email   ___ Mail   ___ A note sent home with my child

If you have more questions, please call:_____

STUDENT and PARENT: WHAT CONCERNS <u>YOU</u>?

This survey helps us to find out what you're thinking about, and what you'd like to see change or improve, or want to organize by yourself. Please answer honestly. It's the only way we can help you. **ALL ANSWERS ARE CONFIDENTIAL.** When you've completed the form, please return it to your child's teacher.

1. HOW DOES YOUR CHILD FEEL ABOUT GOING TO SCHOOL?
   ___ Loves it   ___ Likes it   ___ Dislikes it most of the time   ___ Hates it

2. HOW DOES THE COMMUNITY FEEL ABOUT THE SCHOOL?
   ___ Thinks it's great   ___ Likes it a lot   ___ Thinks it's _____

3. WHAT ARE YOUR CONCERNS ABOUT YOUR CHILD'S SCHOOLING? _____
   _____

4. WHAT DO YOU AND YOUR CHILD DO TOGETHER IN THE EVENINGS? _____
   _____

5. DO YOU HAVE COMMENTS OR QUESTIONS ABOUT:
   The teacher(s) _____ The classroom _____

   The aides _____ The principal _____

   The homework _____ Other _____

6. DURING THE SCHOOL YEAR, IF YOU HAVE A QUESTION OR CONCERN ABOUT YOUR CHILD'S EDUCATION, WHAT DO YOU USUALLY DO?
   ___ Talk to teacher   ___ Go to principal   ___ Talk to other parents   ___ Forget it

7. WHAT QUESTIONS WOULD YOU *REALLY* LIKE TO ASK YOUR CHILD'S TEACHER? OR PRINCIPAL? OR COUNSELOR?
   _____

8. DO YOU FEEL COMFORTABLE CALLING THE TEACHER, PRINCIPAL OR COUNSELOR WITH A PROBLEM? ___ IF NOT, WHY NOT? _____
   _____

9. WHAT WOULD YOU LIKE TO SEE CHANGE AT SCHOOL? _____
   _____
   _____ **(OVER)**

10. ARE YOU AWARE OF PARENT PROGRAMS OFFERED AT THE SCHOOL, LIKE PARENT NIGHTS OR THE PTA?
    ___ Yes   ___ No   ___ Don't really care

11. IF YOU DON'T USUALLY GO, WHY NOT? _____

12. DO YOU THINK PARENT-TEACHER CONFERENCES ARE USEFUL? _____
    IF SO, HOW? _____

13. WHAT DO YOU THINK YOUR CHILD'S STRENGTHS ARE? _____

14. WHAT AREAS DOES YOUR CHILD NEED IMPROVEMENT IN? _____

15. WOULD YOU BE INTERESTED IN SOME IDEAS ON HOW TO HELP YOUR CHILD LEARN?   ___ Yes   ___ No   ___ I'd like to see the ideas first

16. WHAT IS THE BEST WAY TO GET INFORMATION TO YOU?
    ___ Send home with my child   ___ Call me   ___ Mail it   ___ Email....   ___ Send nothing home

17. WOULD YOU BE INTERESTED IN GOING TO MEETINGS WITH OTHER PARENTS ABOUT SPECIAL TOPICS?   ___ Yes   ___ No   ___ I need more information

18. WHAT TOPICS WOULD INTEREST YOU?   ___ Homework Help   ___ Discipline
    ___ Parenting skills   ___ Communication skills   ___ Other

19. WHAT CAN YOU SUGGEST THAT WOULD GET OTHER PARENTS MORE INVOLVED IN SCHOOL? _____

20. WHERE DO YOU THINK THESE MEETINGS SHOULD BE HELD?
    ___ At school   ___ In the library   ___ In a community center
    ___ At a church   ___ At someone's house   ___ Other

21. WHAT DAY, AND TIME OF DAY, IS BEST FOR YOU?
    ___ Before school hours   ___ In the afternoon
    ___ Evenings: ___ Mon ___ Tues ___ Wed ___ Thurs ___ Fri

22. WHEN IS THE BEST TIME TO CONTACT YOU? _____

23. WHAT OTHER KINDS OF EVENTS WOULD BE INTERESTING TO YOU? _____

NEWSLETTER SURVEY

LET US KNOW . . .

As parents and educators, we teach our children together. We make a team that shapes children's lives — which is why we like to keep in touch with you. Our newsletter is one way we do that. We'd like your help in making it as good as it can be. In order to help us do that, please take a few minutes to answer these questions. Circle your answers and return the completed survey to your child's teacher.

- Do you receive our newsletter regularly?   yes / no / sometimes

- Do you actually read it?   yes / no / sometimes / never

- Is it published: too often / not often enough / just enough ?

- Does it provide enough information, such as: dates / schedules / changes / announcements / updates ?

- Does it provide information helpful to parents, such as: parenting tips / ways to teach children at home / resources available when you need help / explanations of programs?

- Does it keep you informed about: educational trends / upcoming issues / new legislation / school board issues ?

- Is our newsletter: easy to read / difficult to understand?

Are the translations: clear / difficult?

- Is material presented in enough time?   yes / no / sometimes

- Would you like artwork or graphics?   more / less / don't care

- Would you like to see students' work?   more / less / don't care

- Do you feel that our newsletter is: interesting / informative / fun / boring / varies with each issue / forget it! / worth doing?

- What can we include or eliminate from our newsletter that would make it more valuable for you?

TEACHER'S QUESTIONS FOR PARENTS

Dear Parents: This questionnaire helps the teacher to know your child better. Your answers are kept strictly confidential. Please return to your child's teacher.

Schoolwork

1. What one thing does your child seem to like the most about school? _____

2. What one thing does your child seem to like the least about school? _____

3. What subject in school does your child have the most trouble in? _____

4. What do you think about your child's progress in school so far? _____

5. Is your child where you thought he/she would be by now? _____

6. Is your child living up to your expectations? _____

7. If you asked yourself if your child could improve in one area above all others, what area would that be? _____

8. If you asked your child the same question, how would he/she answer? _____

9. If you asked your child what would make his or her time at school more stimulating, how do you think he/she would answer? _____

Homework and Learning at Home

10. How often do you help your child with homework? _____

11. How do you feel about helping your child with homework? _____

12. Do you sometimes feel frustrated, angry, or helpless about his or her homework? _____

13. Do you think you'll lose your child's respect if your help isn't adequate? _____

14. Have the homework habits of you and/or your child changed over the years? _____

15. Do you and your child read together?   How often? _____

(OVER)

16. Does your child watch more than two hours of television a day? _____

17. What are some of his or her favorite shows? _____

18. Do you think you and your child communicate well with each other? _____

19. How does your child take it when you correct a mistake or suggest another option? _____

Your Life at Home

20. How do you encourage your child to behave, have good manners, and respect you and other people around him or her? _____

21. How do you think your child gets along with other children:
    At school _____
    At home _____

22. What regular chores or jobs does your child do at home? _____

23. What ways do you validate and praise your child when he/she does something well? _____

24. Does your child seem to thrive on praise? _____

25. What does your child do to relax? _____

26. Do you relax often with your child? _____

27. Do you make sure your child gets enough sleep each school night? _____

28. Do you give your child a substantial breakfast each day? _____

29. Do you genuinely believe in your child? _____

30. Do you respect your child, and show him or her on a regular basis? _____

Name _____
Child's Name _____

Please return to your child's classroom teacher. Remember, all answers are private.

Agreements and Bulletins

Where do they fit in?

Like the Surveys we just looked at, Agreements and Bulletins are part of a two-way communication network between you and the parents you want to reach. Each serves to tell the parent of your concern and your commitment to do the best job you can for the child and the child's parents. Each agreement and bulletin also gives the parent and/or student an opportunity to respond and to offer his or her feedback.

When should these be sent out?

Each Agreement and Bulletin differs. In the examples that follow, for instance, some can be sent in the first week or two of school when you want to take advantage of the initial excitement and eagerness that goes along with the first few weeks of a new grade. Others can go home later, saved for a time when the teacher feels a lack of response from parents, or when he or she senses that there might be some apathy or resentment on the part of students or parents. Each provides a way in which parents can air feelings and may benefit everyone involved.

How are they distributed? How should they look?

You can refer to the beginning of this unit for ways of distribution. Also remember to make everything that you send home as catchy and interesting as you can. Use colored paper, interesting computer fonts or clear hand-writing. Find computerized clip art. Make it arresting enough to engage the child; then he or she will make sure that the parent sees it and responds.

A STUDENT-TEACHER-PARENT AGREEMENT

This agreement helps students, teachers, and parents focus more clearly on the student's growth. When home and school collaborate, the potential for the child's intellectual, emotional, and academic growth is tremendous. This contract assures that everyone is committed to this end result.

A. AS A STUDENT, I AM RESPONSIBLE FOR...
- Respecting and cooperating with all adults in the school.
- Coming to class on time, prepared to work, fed and rested.
- Knowing my classmates have the right to learn without distraction and disruption.
- Respecting others by not using profanity, disrespect, or vandalizing.
- Controlling myself by not running, pushing, or fighting on campus.
- Finishing my homework and assignments to the best of my ability.
- Spending quality time at home, studying and/or reading each day.

Comments:_____

Date_____

Student's signature_____

B. AS A TEACHER, I AM RESPONSIBLE FOR...
- Knowing that students are people who deserve my respect.
- Teaching students in the best way I know how, using the benefits of my education and experience, are continuing to learn and grow.
- Creating a safe and stimulating learning environment.
- Making sure I clearly explain assignments to students.
- Providing honest and understandable evaluations of students' progress and achievement to both students and parents.

Comments:_____

Date_____

Teacher's signature_____

C:. AS A PARENT, I AM RESPONSIBLE FOR...
- Making sure my child is well-fed and rested.
- Providing a homework area and regular schedule so that my child can study or read at home each evening.
- Communicating to my child my respect and love and support.
- Helping my child to understand what his or her responsibilities are to the school, to the family, and to him or herself.

Comments:_____

Date_____

Parent's signature_____

TEACHER'S COMMITMENT TO THE FAMILY

September 1st

Dear Parents and Children of Class #302,

    This is our first week together. It's the first of many weeks in which we'll all be working together on a terrific team. This kind of teamwork allows each of us to do our job — which is to help every child to be all that he or she can truly be.

    This is a tough job, probably one of the toughest jobs there is. There are a lot of mixed signals coming to kids from out there in the real world. Kids have a hard time staying focused on the fact that a good education is vital to their lives.

    I'm going to make some promises to you, and I'll do my very best to keep them. I want to put my energy and trust and strength into giving your child all that I can, so the more that you and your child work with me on keeping these promises, the more we all accomplish. And, the closer we are to keeping your child on the road to success.

I, _____ promise to:
                 (Teacher's Name)

Be respectful of your child by listening, considering feelings and sensitivities, celebrating differences, giving positive messages and constructive feedback.

Be human which means that I won't always be able to be Super Teacher. Once in a while, I may have a bad day.

Be stimulating to your child, develop programs and prepare homework that challenge and excite. My aim is to make each day an adventure in the classroom.

Stay in touch with the family and the student, and to use every means at my disposal to keep this essential triangle connected.

    This is my contract with you. Every contract has two or more people involved. Your involvement along with mine results in our strong commitment to your child's education. All it takes is positive encouragement, genuine listening, and patient attention to your child's academic and behavioral growth.

    Please keep in touch with me in whatever ways you can. Meanwhile, I'm keeping my promises...!

[TEACHER'S SIGNATURE]

TEACHER-TO-FAMILY BULLETIN

STUDENT'S NAME: Jane Doe
WEEK OF: October 22nd
TEACHER'S NAME: Ms. Diaz

THE GREAT NEWS !

Behavior Report: Jane's really helping the younger kids with their work.

Study Report: She's been handing in her homework on time.

Work Habits: Her handwriting is very creative, and her papers are neat.

Great News: We all loved her report on gerbils on Friday.

THE IMPROVEMENT CORNER...

     Jane is such a good student, but she spends so much time chatting with her friend, Sara, that I'm afraid she's missing a lot of what I say to her. She could benefit from concentrating more on her work in the class and less on talking.

PARENT-TO-TEACHER BULLETIN

STUDENT'S NAME: Jane Doe
WEEK OF: September 10th
PARENT(S) NAME: Dorothy Doe

THE GREAT NEWS !
Homework Report:

On three different days this week, Jane started her homework without anyone having to say anything to her. We are really proud of her.

Great News:

Jane has been working on improving her typing skills on the computer and is getting better at it.

THE IMPROVEMENT CORNER....

Jane is really having trouble with remembering to write down her homework assignments from the board. We all talked it over and wonder if you could remind the kids to jot down their homework right before the end of the day. Thanks !

4. Conferences, Conversations and Home Visits
Traditional Approaches Still Work Wonders

The ideal parent involvement program ties in traditional approaches with strategies that are new and innovative. The traditional ways have become traditional because they work. They've proven themselves by achieving their goals, over decades and with thousands of success stories. Some of the traditional methods in parent involvement stem from one-on-one ways of reaching parents through personal contact. Parent-teacher conferences, conversations by phone or in person, and visits to the student's home are three of the most successful and endearing approaches that show parents you care enough to take the time from your own day, are confident about the end results, and that you are willing to put your skills and energy into making sure the experience is successful for everyone involved.

I get by with a little help from my friends.
—The Beatles

Parent-Teacher Conferences

A great opportunity for collaboration

Parent-teacher conferences hold great potential for strengthening a vital bridge between parents, teachers, and students. Sometimes this bridge can be a shaky one, but from this conference can come better communication and deeper understanding of the child's strengths and of the areas that will improve with attention. The players on this team can commit to working together and provide a rock-solid foundation. When a parent doesn't attend the conference, the teacher's initial reaction can be outrage or frustration. But there are many circumstances that might prevent a parent from attending: illness, a constricting work schedule, lack of English skills, intimidation, cultural restrictions, as well as apathy or anger. Rather than give up hope of making this connection between the school and the home, apply some creativity and a bit of extra time. The teacher or school can:

- **Provide telephone time.** For those parents who can't physically make it to school, send a note home with the student, asking to make an appointment for a phone conference. Give the parent the phone number at school. On one to two days a week (specify which days), you'll be available during such-and-such hours for a brief phone conference.

- **Provide a translator.** For parents who can't attend the conference because of lack of English skills, enlist the help of a bilingual parent or staff member.

Initially, the translator can explain the benefits of the conference; then translate during the conference.

- **Make a home visit.** Often, a parent is home bound. If all other efforts have failed to bring the parent into the school, ask the parent if she or he would feel more comfortable if the teacher comes to the house. Work with the principal and counselor; go to the home as a team.

- **Work with community facilities.** If the parent is reluctant to come to the school, talk to a local community group and ask to use space for parent-teacher conferences. Approach the church, senior citizens facility, a youth center, or recreation centers.

- **Work with community groups.** In addition to using their facilities, ask these same groups to work closely with you. Involve parents from a different perspective, and link parents and students with the school. Groups can offer services like transportation, assembly programs, networking, child care, leads on grants and funding, and a wide talent pool.

- **Take a close look at the conference itself.** Do you send out clear information — translated if necessary — with the correct times, dates, etc? Do you involve the students in making sure the notices get home? Do you offer enough hours-options for working parents? When the conference day arrives, do you stay on schedule with the parents? Are your communication skills strong and positive?

- **Send homework pointers to the family.** Ask the parents who attend the conferences and are involved parents to help you put together family games, like word games or math games, as well as other hints on homework, parenting pointers, and a phone list of other parents that have volunteered to help and support.

- **Acknowledge that some parents won't be reached.** There are always those parents that simply refuse to be involved. Don't allow that reality to penalize their child. If the child is old enough, ask if he or she would like a parent volunteer for help, either in tutoring, for language translation, or simply as a "buddy." Give the child — again if age-appropriate — some of the parent information and materials which he or she can use at home or at school.

PARENT-TEACHER CONFERENCE
Guidelines for an Effective Conference

The Parent Knows It's an Effective Conference When the Teacher:

— notifies the parents in plenty of time, and gives the parents options as to times they can come.
— provides translators when needed for each parent.
— keeps the schedule running on time.
— or the school has made provisions for child care during the conferences.
— is well-organized.
— treats the student as an individual and shows a genuine interest in him or her.
— focuses in on the positive aspects of the child and points them out to the parents and student.
— is receptive and not defensive about the parent's questions.
— keeps the conference on target and doesn't ramble or move off into social conversation.
— has workable suggestions and ways that the child can be helped, in school and at home.

The Teacher Knows It's an Effective Conference When the Parent:

— confirms her/his appointment time.
— arrives shortly before his or her time.
— comes with a list of questions for the teacher.
— understands that the teacher places the welfare of the child as a high priority.
— wants to work with the teacher and school as part of a team, and doesn't want to be divisive.
— is friendly and receptive, and keeps the conference solely focused on the child.
— takes notes or listens very carefully.
— doesn't pontificate, blame or take over the conference.
— has clearly thought about her/his child's accomplishments.
— wants a schedule or a plan of action for the parent-teacher team.
— genuinely thanks the teacher.

WELCOME TO THE GREENFIELD ELEMENTARY
PARENT-TEACHER CONFERENCE

October 15, 20___

Welcome to all Greenfield Elementary Parents !

    In two weeks, we'll be hosting our semi-annual Parent-Teacher conferences. It is so important that you attend that we're offering two different options: On October 29th, your child's teachers will be available from 3 to 8 pm. On October 30th, school will be shortened to a half-day, to make it possible for parents to come from 12 noon to 6 p.m.

    Please make all efforts to come. It is very important to your child's teachers that they have the opportunity to meet you and to talk about areas of interest. It makes a world of difference to everyone involved.

I'm looking forward to seeing you then !!

Sincerely,

[SIGNED BY PRINCIPAL OR INDIVIDUAL TEACHER]

THE BEST TIME(S) FOR ME TO COME ARE:
(Please check as many OPTIONS as possible}

October 29th: ___ 3-4   ___ 4-5   ___ 5-6   ___ 6-7   ___ 7-8

October 30th: ___ 12-1   ___ 1-2   ___ 2-3   ___ 3-4   ___ 4-5   ___ 5-6

Name _____ Phone _____

Email _____

Child's Name(s) _____ Class _____

_____ Class _____

_____ Class _____

Please RETURN THIS form to the Classroom teacher or the Principal...
Thank you!

I'M EXCITED ABOUT MEETING YOU !

October,

Hello Parents!

Our parent-teacher conference is coming up in less than two weeks, and I'm really looking forward to it. I'll be meeting many of you for the first time. There are a lot of parents to meet, and I have only 15 minutes for the family of each student. I want to make the most of our time together. Attached, you'll find some suggested questions you can ask me during the conference. Please look over the list. Some of the questions may work for you, others will spark your own questions. The main idea is that we're here to talk about your child, my student, and ways that we can work together!

Sincerely,

[Teacher's name printed]

[Teacher's signature]

Questions the Parent Can Ask the Teacher in the Conference:

—How well does my child get along with other kids? With you, the teacher? With staff and aides?

—What areas of schoolwork is my child strong in?

—What areas of schoolwork does my child need work in?

—Does it matter that my child is not very developed in some or many areas that other children seem to have no problems in?

—Do you think my child is working up to her/his abilities?

—How does my child express his or her emotions, like anger or frustration?

—What are some of the positive things my child does in class?

—What ways do you as the teacher reward or punish behaviors?

—Does my child work better with other children or alone?

—How do you grade your students?

—What things can I do at home to help my child?

—How much homework help do you think the parents should give?

—How much time should my child be spending on homework each night?

—Do you think my child's homework could use some improvement?

—What are your requirements for homework being on time?

—What consequences do the children face when homework is late?

—What can we do together to create a positive collaboration and team, and stay excited about working for the growth of my child?

Parent Conversations and Home Visits

What's the difference?

Actually, there are as many similarities as there are differences in conversations and home visits. Both give information and insights into the child's family and home life as well as neighborhoods and communities. Both are conducted and designed by people who care, and by people who want to see children become lifelong learners, and who appreciate the role of parents in this endeavor.

The differences are spatial more than anything. A conversation and home visit may include the same questions asked by the same person, with the same goal in mind. A conversation usually happens in the school, in the office of either a teacher, counselor, or principal, or in the parents' room. A home visit usually takes place in the home of the child or family of the child. Many parents are reluctant to come into an environment as intimidating to them as a school can be. They are too shy to talk easily, or can't speak the language at all and need an interpreter, often a family member or their own child. They feel more at ease at home, where they can open up and share their feelings or concerns.

All can hear, but only the sensitive can understand.
—Kahlil Gibran

The affirmation makes a big difference

By caring enough to reach out to the parent, you are sending a strong signal. That signal says that there are people who care — about the child and the parent. You care enough to take your own time to listen, to come into someone else's territory. That's a commitment that doesn't go unnoticed.

When a parent makes it clear that visitors aren't welcome, but is equally adamant about avoiding the school, think of another place that's more comfortable for the parent. A church, perhaps, or a community center, senior citizens center, or day-care center. Or meet at a diner or nice restaurant if both people can afford that. Find a place that's not threatening.

Preparation takes some forethought.

- **Be warm and friendly.** This isn't a work-related conversation, it's a dialogue between two people who care about the same child. Be informal and friendly, listen attentively and actively. Let the parent do most of the talking unless he or she has specific questions that require your answers.

- **Go prepared.** Have a list of questions concerning issues related to home and school. Put them in order of priority in case the parent is interrupted or abruptly ends the visit or conversation. Don't let the session go too long unless the parent really wants to continue.

- **Be positive.** Focus on the positive — and genuine — aspects of the child. Find things you really like or admire about the child. Even if you have criticisms, keep them in a positive vein. You don't have to figure it all out in one visit or conversation.

Making Phone Calls Home to Parents

Parents are your best ally

Parents are the most important people in a child's life. As an educator, counselor, community member, or another parent, you need the parent's strong commitment before you can both work together successfully. One of the better ways of getting through to a parent is to make a call home and set a positive tone that opens a successful school year. Make a point of calling each family once every 6 to 8 weeks, more often if possible.

Keep it positive

Keep the calls brief and chatty — and be positive. Being positive is the most important aspect to the call, especially if the teacher has had problems with the child, or if the child is having trouble now. By establishing a good relationship with the parent, it's not so difficult to call later if a problem does come up. The parent is more likely to work with you in solving the problem.

Some pointers:
- **Introduction.** Tell the parent who you are, and ask if it's a good time to chat. If not, set up a time that works for both of you. Assure the parent there's nothing wrong and it's okay to relax! Keep the discussion friendly, informal, and unintimidating. Make it conversational.

- **Look for the positive.** Find some aspects about the student that are genuinely positive. These can be about the student's academic abilities, athletic accomplishments, behavior in the classroom and around school, specifics about her good deeds or interactions, or talents like drawing, singing, or comedic skills.

- **Encourage the child.** Encourage the parent to share your conversation with the student. This way, the child knows that both his teacher and parent have exchanged positive input about him.

- **Encourage the parent.** Get her to talk about anything she feels is important. Don't draw the conversation out for very long. Tell the parent she can always make an appointment to talk to the teacher.

- **Summarize.** In a very informal way, give a quick reflection of the conversation. "I'm glad you've noticed that Jewel has really gotten more creative in her writing. If you need any more help in getting into that ESL class, by the way, just call me and I'll do what I can."

- **Sign off.** Say goodbye after saying something like, "Give my best to (child and/or spouse and/or sibling)"

A PHONE CALL TO THE CHILD'S HOME
A Suggested Script

"Hello, is this Carmen's (mother/father)? I'm _(caller's name)_ and I'm calling from Carmen's school to get some information, if you've got a few moments. If this is a bad time, I can call back, but it should only take a couple minutes.

"Everything you tell me is totally confidential, by the way. "I'll ask you questions and you answer to anything that fits. Ready?"

1. Do you receive the school newsletter?
   Do you read it?
   ___ always   ___ frequently   ___ sometimes   ___ never

2. Are there any changes you'd suggest to improve the newsletter?

3. What are some of the ways your get your information about the school?
   ___ from my child   ___ from his or her friends   ___ from the teacher
   ___ from TV   ___ from the school paper   ___ from the local newspaper
   ___ from the principal   ___ from community centers   ___ from church
   ___ from local businesses
   Other sources: _____

4. Would you like to have more information about the school's:
   ___ discipline policy   ___ homework policy   ___ special needs classes
   ___ gifted class   ___ parent involvement programs
   ___ curriculum for your child's class   ___ testing

5. What are some other things at school that you'd like to know more about?

6. Would you like the school to try harder to keep you informed?

7. Would you be interested in joining a parent's group or PTA?

8. Did you go to the last parent-teacher meeting?   Why not?
   or How did it go?

9. Do you have regular contact with your child's teacher? Principal?

10. Does your child have problems you feel the teacher isn't addressing?

11. How would you improve the school in general?

Thank you so much, Ms./Mr._____This really helps the school get an idea of what the parents and students want for the school. Have a good night.

5. Asking Parents to Volunteer at School

What does the future look like for you?

We've been looking at ways to keep parents receptive and their interests alive. These things are important — but what are your long-range plans for these parents? Do you just want to keep them receptive, or do you want them to actively participate in the classroom? You need to draw up a blueprint. What do you want them to do, and when? Get them involved by delegating jobs.

THE CLASSROOM: Involve parents in such things as:
- Tutoring math, spelling, reading, a language.
- Speaking to the class about travel, a skill, an adventure, a job.
- Story-telling tales of their culture, religion, experiences, family memories.
- Art projects, like designing a miniature city, making a quilt, or a cultural mural
- Culture walks through historic neighborhoods, in museums, botanical gardens, old parts of town
- Organizing the classroom, baking for class fund-raiser, going on field trips

SCHOOL WIDE: The parents may get involved in:
- Working with students in the cafeteria or playground.
- Working with students on cleaning up the school grounds, and on beautification projects for the neighborhood.
- Vocational training for various classes or individuals.
- Volunteering for the school newspaper.

Learning should be an invitation, not an assignment.
—Jerome Harste

Guidelines for Classroom Volunteers

A CLASSROOM VOLUNTEER:
- Respects and enjoys working with all the children not just his or her own.
- Gives attention, focus and patience to children, individually and in groups.
- Views his or her work with children as important.
- Develops trust with children, teachers, and parents.

A CLASSROOM VOLUNTEER CAN:
- Tutor students in reading, spelling, science, math, languages, homework, other subjects and areas.
- Read to or be read to by children.
- Correct papers and exams.
- Help the teacher take the children to different school areas or on class or school trips, to museums, and on walking tours.
- Encourage writing and self-expression in individual groups.
- Make materials for class plays, projects, and special programs.
- Work with children to write and create projects.

A CLASSROOM VOLUNTEER CAN ALSO:
- Attend classes — when available — that train him or her for more effective volunteering skills or requirements.
- Ask for specific assignments from the volunteer coordinator.
- Be aware of responsibilities. Show up on time, call when late or when absent.

- If his or her time is limited, find creative options. Make calls from work, stuff envelopes one hour a week, design flyers at home.

A CLASSROOM VOLUNTEER MAKES A DIFFERENCE WHEN HE OR SHE:
- Shares a close and focused block of time with the child.
- Gives the teacher effective support and better quality time.
- Grows alongside the students and teachers as she or he gains self-esteem, leadership skills, decision-making options.
- Provides a valuable link between school and community.

A Volunteer Checklist
for First-time Volunteers

Thank you for volunteering to help us. Your time, energy, skills and talents make a real difference between our success and failure!

You can be even more effective if you know what's expected of you. Please look over the following guidelines before you begin:

- Do you know what your group expects you to do?

- Are there specific rooms that you'll be working in? Do you know where they are?

- Do you know the people you'll be working with?

- What days of the week are you expected to work? What times during those days can you commit to?

- Do you have the names, phone numbers, and email addresses of the people with whom you'll be working?

- If you have a problem concerning your responsibilities, or any interpersonal difficulties, do you know with whom you can discuss them?

- Are you responsible for keeping any ongoing records, submitting expenses or other similar record-keeping?

- Will you be using any equipment, such as a copier, that you need specific instructions in using?

- Are there supplies you'll need to know where to find?

- Are you aware of giving students and your co-volunteers positive encouragement, validation, and respect?

- Are you committed to working to the best of your abilities and to achieving a job you can be proud of?

Thanks again - and welcome!

Community Volunteer Survey
Sponsored by The Main St. School

Our school is an important part of the community — and so are you! If you have some extra time and energy, we encourage you to join us. There is so much to do and there are many interesting students, teachers, and parents in our school who want to meet you and work alongside you. **We can improve our community and our children's lives by working together** !

Name _____ Work Phone _____

Address _____ Home Phone _____

Email Address _____

I CAN HELP IN THESE WAYS: (CHECK AS MANY AS YOU LIKE)
___ Help in the office: ___Type ___Xerox ___Word processing ___Filing ___Sorting
___ Read aloud to children: ___in classrooms ___in assembly ___in other language
___ Help supervise children: ___in lunchroom ___on playground ___on break
 ___before school ___after school
___ Listen to and tutor children: ___in reading ___in math ___in spelling
 ___in science
In other areas, like: _____
___ Help in the library ___ Help in audio/visual room ___ Help with newsletter
___ Help make phone calls ___ Help children with oral histories ___ Help make crafts
 or art projects
___ Help beautify school: ___hallways and bulletin boards ___grounds
 ___auditorium
Other areas are: _____

I'D BE GLAD TO SHARE WITH PARENTS OR TEACHERS:
___ Information about my career or job which is: _____
___ Show students: _____
___ Talk to students about foreign travel and interesting places, like: _____
___ Talk about and demonstrate my special hobby, which is: _____
___ Give introductory vocational training in: _____
___ Become involved in a mentoring project, working one-on-one with a student who shows interests or talents similar to my own.
___ Demonstrate or talk about: ___Drama ___Writing ___Television ___Art ___Ceramics
 ___Sketching ___Cooking ___Music ___Design ___Fabric ___Sports, like: _____
Other subjects: _____

I'D LIKE TO WORK WITH:
___ Pre-schoolers ___ Kindergarten ___1-3 grades ___ 4-6 grades ___ Middle school
___ High school ___ Parents ___ Teachers ___ Administrators ___ Elderly volunteers
___ Community volunteers

FACILITATOR: PLEASE SEND COMPLETED FORM TO:
 Main St. School - c/o Ms. Reyes - 789 Main St. - Our Town, USA

Teacher's Request for Classroom Volunteer

I NEED THE HELP OF A VOLUNTEER FOR THE FOLLOWING:

In the **classroom.** I need someone to help me: _____

_____

I need this person's help on this day(s): _____

During these times: _____

I also need another volunteer to: _____

On this day(s): During these times: _____

I could use some help with the following **clerical** jobs:
___ Keyboarding   ___ Word processing   ___ Organizing the classroom
___ Making copies

Other: _____

I need assistance in **art projects:** _____

_____

I need help in these **other areas:** _____

_____

Extra comments on this request: _____

_____

_____

TEACHER'S NAME: _____   **DATE** _____

SUBJECT: _____   **ROOM** _____

Please return this request form with your child or place it in the Volunteer Box in the Office. Thank you....

6. Ideas for Social Gatherings, Projects, and Events

Task involvement is a mighty socializer

When people do things together, this involvement in a shared, common task brings them closer to one another. Parents, too, can feel shy or embarrassed around other parents with whom the only common thread is that of having children. Often parents stay away from groups of other parents because they feel they have so little in common.

Especially in culturally diverse groups, task involvement makes a considerable difference when bringing parents into a group. In this unit, we've included a wide range of ideas on social events and gatherings, as well as project ideas — like making a parents' room and a welcoming video, suggestions for publishing an exciting and informative newsletter, and tips for conducting parent workshops.

A "GETTING TO KNOW YOU" PARTY

This party is geared for early fall, right after school has started and things have settled down a bit. The purpose is to have fun, and create an opportunity for parents and teachers, the principal, counselor and other staff to get to know each other.

Ask local restaurants to contribute the food for the event. Or, food can be cooked by some of the parents, or by all, as in a potluck dinner. But, make sure that food is good, plentiful, and culturally appropriate to your parents. Offer rewards like door prizes of cash or gift certificates. Make sure everyone fills out and wears a name tag listing their name, their children's names.

Games can be played, like bingo or roulette. Or have a game-theme night, with different tables set up for chess, checkers, and cards. Such games bring people together and are relaxing for many. Other people, who are not game players, can talk and eat. Don't let the party go for more than three hours.

"MAKE AND TAKE" PARTIES

The parents work together with the children, teachers, and other parents in creating projects they can take home with them. Especially geared to holidays, the options are endless: Plant seedlings in flower pots that you've made and decorated together. Then, give the potted plants as gifts. Make masks, and write stories that tell about them. Decorate cookies, cupcakes, and cakes.

THE FAMILY-TREE BOOK PARTY

The child — with the encouragement and direction from the parent — interviews an older member of her family. She makes a family tree and brief history of the family. The book can include stories, genealogy, photographs, drawings, moments to remember, interviews with neighborhood people about their memories of your family or of the neighborhood. The book can have additional blank pages so that adding to the scrapbook is an ongoing family activity.

The individual class — or the whole school — plans an evening on which they share and talk about their own books with other families. A few children make special presentations and talk about the experience of making their book.

PARENTS' NIGHT OUT

This is an event just for parents — no children allowed. By having no agenda other than enjoying themselves, parents can chat with other parents, with teachers and the principal, while eating a delicious meal and not having to deal with cooking or cleaning up.

Ask a local restaurant if it will donate part (or all) of the costs of the dinners, in return for which the restaurant will receive thanks in the school newsletter or be recognized by the PTA in some way that generates good will. Or, ask the parents to each pay their share, or request that the PTA partially fund the dinner.

Send out hand-written invitations, and follow up with phone calls. Arrange for child care by asking some parents to relinquish their evening. Or, pay several baby-sitters to watch the children at school or in another safe location. Decorate the site of the event like a jazz club, or in some way that recognizes parents as "grown ups" entitled to an evening out.

MULTICULTURAL CELEBRATION HANDBOOK

Especially useful in a culturally-diverse environment in which there is a wide cultural span. Parents and children compile a book of customs and holidays representing the students and/or staff. Parents and children share them with other parents and students, learning more about each other.

BREAKFAST WITH THE PRINCIPAL

Food is a great attraction for everyone. It relaxes most people to share a meal and often creates a more intimate and trusting time together. You can develop a specific agenda, such as a proposed plan of action by the PTA, or simply use the time to relax together and chat.

Consider having a bagel and cream cheese or pancake breakfast in the school cafeteria once a year with all the parents together. Or hold a monthly affair with a group of 10-20 parents, each time bringing together a new group of parents for lunch or dinner. Send out for pizza, bring potluck dishes, or order up a box lunch.

CHILDREN'S ART GALLERY

Create a space in the building that's a permanent art gallery:

- —Change the exhibits on a regular basis.
- —Represent individual child artists, classes, grades, or other groupings.
- —Establish themes, such as multi-cultural, book heroes and heroines, favorite places, maps, masks, and curriculum subjects.
- —Include a section of the board for the contributions of teachers and parents.

NEIGHBORHOOD CLEAN-UP

With other parents, students, teachers, and community members, organize a committee to clean up and beautify the school, school grounds, and/or the neighborhood.

START A SINGLE-PARENT CLUB

Open to mothers and fathers who are single, this club meets every week or two, or monthly, so that members can share the pros and cons of being a single parent and network with other parents.

ORGANIZE A FUND-RAISING COMMITTEE

This committee does one thing — it brainstorms ways to raise money, finds volunteers to carry out selected plans, and raises the money. Usually, another committee allocates the funds.

PROVIDE TRANSLATORS

Many schools need growing numbers of parents, family members, even students, to act as translators in classrooms, at PTA meetings, and for the school newsletter. Set up a rotating number of parents or community members who are willing to participate.

HELP OUT BEFORE OR AFTER SCHOOL

The hour before and the hour or two after school can almost always use extra volunteers. Assign them to help with breakfast and bus arrivals in the morning, to work with after-school groups, tutor children, and help organize in the school library.

BE PART OF THE GRADUATION COMMITTEE

At any grade level, children love graduations and ceremonies. From a balloon party to tasseled caps, gowns, and the school band, children deserve these positive rituals.

COLLECT USED ITEMS

Organize a group event at which used sports equipment, computers and printers, books, toys, and learning tools can be sold. Advertise heavily in local newspapers. Have the kids make up posters. Distribute flyers.

REQUEST REPRESENTATIVES/ DELEGATES

Find parents who are willing to designate a specific time each month to attend meetings of parents' groups, parenting conferences, and workshops. As representatives from and to the school, they can bring back valuable information — and make the school look good.

ORGANIZE A NEWSLETTER

Represent the PTA, the school, and the community. Have students, teachers, and parents write columns. Get local businesses to buy ads. Set up an attractive catchy logo. Include photos and drawings if possible. Distribute the newsletter to the children on a regular basis. Run it off on brightly colored paper. Make it interesting to the children so they'll read it themselves, as well as share it with their families.

HOLD A FLEA MARKET

On school grounds, in the lunchroom, gym, or auditorium, display items donated from parents, teachers, and community members. Offer space and tables to local vendors for a small fee. Have local restaurant owners donate food or sell it to you very cheaply. Advertise, and distribute flyers. Try to specialize: Feature marbles, baseball cards, miniatures, books.

COACH SCHOOL GAMES

Most schools can always use extra help in track, basketball, soccer, football, and softball. Many schools don't have much of a sports program, and might welcome help organizing one.

ORGANIZE A HALLOWED HALLS PROGRAM

With the principal and the teachers, pinpoint specific hallways that are dreary and need some attention. Have a contest, asking the kids for suggestions as to what the hallways need. Give the winning class a pizza or ice cream, and make the hallways fun.

CREATE FRIENDS OF THE LIBRARY

Invite parents and students to work together during lunch hours, or before or after school. With the librarian, have the team sort books, checking their condition, then catalog and log them. Have the same group organize a Book Fair, Author's Week, and Storytelling Hours — all to raise money for books.

START A MOTHERS' MONTHLY MEETING

All moms experience those rushes of panic, resentment, and loss of control. Most moms think they're the only ones who do. When mothers talk it out, they grow. Make it a safe environment where moms feel free to share their feelings.

ORGANIZE AN AFTER-SCHOOL PROGRAM

From one to five days a week, parents, students, and community members can band together and pool their talents to create and run a thriving and stimulating after-school program. This can include sports programs, homework help, arts and crafts, nature walks, and can be paid for by moderate parent and school donations.

CREATE A VOLUNTEER TUTOR PROGRAM

Find parents who are knowledgeable or skilled in specific areas such as math, science, literature, and languages. Other parents are necessary as in-class helpers, working one-on-one with individual children, or speaking to the class on a regular basis.

DEVELOP A COMMUNITY OUTREACH GROUP

Keep in touch with the people and the events in the school's community. Talk to the people in various community centers, like teen rap groups and senior citizens groups. Go to the pastors or rabbis of local centers of worship. Ask all these community groups what they need. Tell them the needs of the school. Try to identify collaboration possibilities.

START A SCOUT GROUP

With either a parent or community member as leader, start a Girl Scout, Boy Scout and/or Brownie troop. The groups supply rules, guidelines, and healthy outlets. They emphasize good ethics and strong values, as well as teach valuable skills.

ORGANIZE A NUTRITION COMMITTEE

With student representatives, parents, teachers, and the head dietitian of the school lunch room, create a watchdog committee. Make sure the menu is posted weekly. Work with the lunchroom to provide nutritious and tasty food. Do your part to end childhood obesity. Bring the program into the home in whatever ways possible

START HOLIDAY COMMITTEES

Especially in culturally diverse schools, the holiday committees make sure that all holidays are represented — in classroom themes, with events, by hallway displays, assemblies, cards, and activities. Provide the appropriate music, costumes, food, and observe customs.

CREATE A HOSPITALITY GROUP

For PTA meetings, parent events, and activities, this group of parents provides coffee, tea, milk, cookies or cake, sliced fruit, and/or vegetables, and more substantial food when the occasion calls for it. They organize the buying of supplies, the set-up, supervision, and final clean up.

THROW A "THANK YOU" PARTY

At the end of the school year, give a party that says thanks to all volunteers, students, teachers, school personnel and members of the community who have contributed time, money, and skills. Hold this "Thank You" party at school (an hour of cake and ice cream), or schedule it in the evening at a local restaurant. Distribute a nicely printed list of the volunteers. Give out small prizes, if possible.

HAVE A SATURDAY CLUB

This group is for parents who work during the week and would like to team up to take their children on various trips: to ball games, museums, boat excursions, fishing, hiking, swimming, etc.

ORGANIZE A SCIENCE FAIR

With the science teachers, and other classroom teachers, work with the students on a theme for a Science Fair. The children can submit experiments, drawings, and mock-ups. Open the exhibit to all students and parents, and award prizes or certificates.

HOST A POTLUCK DINNER

Do it once or repeat the event monthly. Ask families to bring dishes, prearranged to evenly distribute courses and selections. Occasionally announce a theme: food from Mexico or China, food cooked without meat, decorated food, etc.

BEGIN AN ARTS AND CRAFTS CLUB

Once a week, or twice a month, these parents (and students) meet to create arts and crafts, like embroidery, quilts, ceramics, potholders, and sketches. The meetings are fun, and the results can be sold at a special event.

ORGANIZE A FLYER COMMITTEE

Every event, activity, and on-going fund raiser needs an effective, eye-catching flyer. Find people who can draw, typeset, do word processing and desktop publishing. One or two people can write copy, adding all pertinent information. Make the flyers interesting! (See page 129 for more information.)

HAVE A VALENTINE'S PARTY FOR ADULTS

Give parents a rare chance to have a night alone — and a romantic one at that. Find a local nightclub or restaurant with private rooms and arrange for dinner and dancing for couples at a reasonable group rate. Arrange for baby sitting, if possible. Create some activities that promote affection and intimacy.

LAUNCH A PRE-TEEN AND/OR TEEN SUPPORT GROUP

Peer counseling is often the best way to help young adults face their problems and deal with them. And when they talk to each other, they feel more confident, less plagued by doubts. Hold these meetings weekly, after school and on campus, or at someone's home in the early evening.

The Red Carpet Video

Send a positive welcoming message to in-coming parents and new students by showing them a video about the school, made by the students themselves, and supervised by the teachers and the principal.

Not only is video an exciting way of presenting information, it's also the most arresting media vehicle for a child or parent. Videos are relatively cheap to produce, and laying different languages onto the audio track is easy. Most exciting, video gives the students a chance to explore their school, get involved in several different subjects, and work closely with other children, teachers, parents, and, often, community members. The result: a video that informs and entertains new students, reassuring them that their new school is going to provide many positive experiences. For schools serving minority students, the video presentation and translation should serve to demonstrate that language and cultural barriers can be broken down through collaborative team efforts.

The Steps for Making a Video

- **Plan.** In preparing for the video, the planning committee must decide what is important. What do you want to get across: curriculum? students? the library? the gym? the teachers' attitudes? Whom do you want to interview: the principal, students, teachers, custodian or staff? Do you want to convey humor, serious information, or both? Length-wise, a video is effective at 3 to 5 minutes, boring after 10 minutes.

- **Write.** The script committee takes the decisions made by the planning committee and uses them to write the script. The script needs to flow. It needs a beginning, a middle and a positive ending. Remember that the script may need to be translated into other languages, so keep it simple.

- **Budget.** Work out the cost for a 5- to 10-minute video tape. Figure in costs of renting equipment, if needed, buying plenty of video capacity, and any special extras: editing time to take out unwanted footage, any electronic graphics titles, music, and special effects, such as freeze frames.

- **Produce.** This is the task of the production team. Working from the script and the budget, assess what you'll need to actually video the script. What wardrobe: clothes, shoes, changes of clothes? Do you need special makeup or hair? How about stunts? Where will you record, and in how many different locations? Does your area require film/video permits to tape outside on public property? Schedule times. For example, you may need to shoot Teacher X in the lunchroom at noon, or the principal at the assembly next Friday at 9:30 a.m. Do you want to use community people who take an active part in the school? Whom? Contact and schedule them. Line up translators — parents from the school or people from the community — who will record in different languages over the videotape.

- **Rehearse.** Several things may need to be practiced prior to the recording: any lines said by actors, use of the videotape camera equipment, experiments with lights and audio/sound mikes, wardrobe and hair, and any stunts or special effects.

- **Shoot the project.** Your video camera operator should be an adult, student, or team of students with prior experience operating the equipment. Someone with some experience or natural talent for directing stands in charge, directing the crew and the actors.

He or she has an assistant to help delegate chores and another helper to takes notes: "The basketball game was shot on the videocassette drive marked X." "The camera person shot the teacher saying the same line 4 ways, but the second take was the best."

- **Post-produce the video.** Using the talents of a parent, student, or teacher who can edit the materials, complete all editing and special graphics or effects, like freezing a frame, putting pictures in a box, music over, sound effects, adding video of still pictures, or flat art work. How many copies do you need to order? Are they just for show, or are they for sale to the general school public? Do they need sleeve and labels? If yes, prepare artwork for duplication.

Need a simpler version...?

Many schools don't have the components listed above, and simply want to make a fun home video — with no editing or fancy audio recording in different languages — that shows the school, the students, and the teachers in a good light.

Simply go over the format above and cross out the aspects you won't be doing at your school. What you *will* need to do is to plan the video well. It must be:

- **Sequential.** When you or the students actually begin to shoot your video, you have little room for error. Without the luxury of editing, you must be prepared to take the video from beginning to end.

- **Well-rehearsed.** Because you have such a small margin for error, go over lines, rehearse speeches, get your "actors" to feel comfortable with what they'll be doing.

- **Short.** Especially in a video with few special effects or with minimal audio or video quality, keep it short and sweet.

- **A team effort.** Make sure that all the people involved are working well together, and that all agree from the beginning on what they want the final tape to achieve. Agreement makes the project run smoothly.

Creating a Welcoming Parents' Room

Call it a parents' room, resource center, or family room

Whatever you call this space in your school, make it a warm, welcoming environment in which parents can relax and network. A parents' room is a place to share, to receive and exchange valuable information. Ideally, it is a "home away from home," with a coffee pot, a small refrigerator, and comfortable chairs and desks. A corner with toys, books, and coloring books is set up for preschoolers who come to the room with their parents during school. A bookcase offers books and resources for parents to borrow.

A parents' room is a place where parents can:
- Share feelings and adult conversation with other parents, community members, and school staff.
- Organize a lending library, featuring information on subjects like parenting, the school and school district, communication, conflict-resolution, discipline, AIDS, health issues, vocational-training resources, adult education classes, etc.
- Get up-dated flyers and brochures on school-related events.
- Hold classes for other parents on a variety of subjects, depending on the needs and desires of the group.
- Read to children and work with them individually.

- Organize and store things needed for events, like games, posters, prizes, and small games for the Spring Fair.
- Have a cup of coffee and eat lunch quietly with other parents.
- Take care of class/parent business, such as preparing newsletters, copying them on the copy machine, and bundling them for distribution.
- Exchange used toys, children's books, and clothing.

Ideally, to create a welcoming parents' room, you need:
- A space that's accessible to strollers, wheel chairs, and storage of boxes that come regularly to a parents' group or PTA.
- A room that has light and windows, a door that locks to secure goods, cabinets that can store supplies, food, and other things found in a parents' room.
- Chairs and a desk or two; folding chairs for meetings; a table for collating flyers and newsletters; rugs, small chairs, and supplies for preschoolers; a coffee pot and small refrigerator; a copy machine and typewriter; a camera or two for recording school events; a computer and printer.
- A group of parents who volunteer to be in the room at regular and posted times and who greet and welcome other parents, or help individuals find things they need in the room. Make sure one of the volunteers speaks an appropriate second language.

Grandpeople's Day

One of the solid links in the school-home connection comes from the elderly people in our families and communities. These grandparents, great aunts and uncles, neighbors, senior citizen groups, and older family friends provide a bridge to the students' past — and their futures.

The Goal of Grandpeople's Day:

Growing up is unique for everyone. Yet each generation has its differences and similarities. By sharing them, everyone involved has a golden opportunity to learn more about others — and about themselves.

Step One: Organizing the Day

A committee is formed from representatives of the parents' group, the student body, and the teachers. The committee:

- Determines a day to hold the event.

- Contacts several community groups and samples a few of the elderly members to determine whether the event is welcomed, and if the date is acceptable.

- Decides on a theme and activities, as well as refreshments, time and place, tables and chairs, accommodations for people who need ramps and other assistive services/devices.

- Decides on food: simple snacks or a meal? Bring your own, potluck, donated, or cooked by the people sponsoring the event.

Treat children as though they already are the people they are capable of becoming.
—Haim Ginott

- Designs an invitation which asks elderly guests:
    — to bring pictures of themselves when they were young.
    — if they mind being interviewed by students.
    — to think about similarities and differences between their youth and today's young people.
    — to come with their minds open to learning about young people as well as talking to them.

Students and teachers, and/or parents, collaborate to prepare a workable agenda for the event. They can prepare interview questions, activities, and brainstorming topics; write and produce short plays; read aloud their thoughts, poems, short stories about their perceptions of their grandparents and other elderly people, or what they think it was like back in "the olden days."

Contact the local newspaper, the editor of the school newsletter, and community bulletins, and let them know about the event.

Step Two: The Day of the Event

Length of the Event:
The event is not a long one, ideally 2 hours maximum.

The Setting:
The setting is a place that's comfortable, well-lit and ventilated. Snacks, coffee, and water are provided. Chairs or benches are comfortable. Extra cushions can be brought in for the day. Depending on the weather and how many people are attending, the event can take place:

- in an auditorium
- outdoors on the school grounds
- in individual classrooms
- in the school library

Suggested Activities:
- **Musical revue.** The school band, chorus, or individual classes play or sing songs from earlier generations.

- **Sharing Circle.** Break children up into groups of 10, each with an additional adult and a grandperson. Each group is asked to talk about the topic, "As a Child, My Favorite Place to Go Was/Is..." Each person in the group talks about the topic. Then, the grandperson shows his or her pictures and shares remembrances of when he/she was in school.

- **Have a picnic.** Participants can bring their own lunch/dinner, share in a potluck meal, or arrange for food to be provided by local restaurants.

- **Take photographs.** Pose various people together, with each group having representatives from as many generations as possible.

- **Compare.** In discussion groups or classroom groups (depending on the number of participants), compare and discuss:
    —Customs and behavior
    —Parenting
    —Music, arts, film, television
    —Dress and clothing, styles and fads
    —Technology
    —Jobs and careers, realities and aspirations
    —Education
    —Food and cooking
    —Games and play

- **Create permanent displays.** Grandpeople and students work together, along with a supervising teacher or parent, to create an artistic representation of both their lives.
    —A mural
    —A collage of photographs and drawings
    —A videotape
    —A verbally-illustrated oral history on audio tape
    —A sculpture done with paper maché, wire, or scraps
    —A quilt

This display can be finished on Grandpeople's Day, or the older people can return on a regular basis to complete the project with the students.

- **The young talk to the old.** The children prepare individual ways to tell the grandpeople about themselves. Using a picture, poem, story, or music, they give their point of view about being a young person in today's world. The teachers invite the grandpeople to a mini-lesson in the classroom. This lesson can be reading, math, science, computers. Let the grandpeople glimpse how different the classrooms of today really are.

- **Create a Grandpeople Pen Pals Club.** The students and the grandpeople who are willing can make a pact to continue communicating. They can write to or email one another, call on the phone regularly, send photographs and hand-drawn pictures, and find other ways of saying, "hello, this is who I am, and I care." Ideally, the grandperson should not be related to the child he/she is paired with. Non-related partners are better suited to giving each other new ideas and perspectives.

- **Say thanks to the grandpeople.** Assign each class to write short notes to all the people who attended. Have each student design and sign a separate note.

Guidelines for a School Newsletter

The school newsletter is a flowing conduit

The newsletter, or bulletin, uses a variety of exciting and stimulating ways to get information to, and from, parents, students and teachers in a school. Translate when possible, or have a regular column in another language. For a newsletter to be really effective and desirable, it should be distributed regularly, even if it is printed rather infrequently. Every 4-6 weeks keeps the news current and the readership happy.

Some of the ways a newsletter communicates are:

- Feature articles by students, teachers, parents, and community members on classroom activities, school-wide and community news.

- Information for students, parents, and teachers about school- or education-related subjects, like homework tips and discipline alternatives.

- Announcement of up-coming events, in the class and school.

- Articles reprinted from other sources.

- Book reviews, written by students.

- Regular columns; letters or messages from the Principal, parent-group President and Treasurer, school counselor, head of the Class Parent Program, and district Superintendent.

- A Calendar of Events, including up-coming holiday fairs, raffles, parent workshops and seminars; PTA or parent group meetings; parent-teacher conference; open school week; book fair.
- Important phone numbers of people in the school and community.
- Photographs, drawings, collages, and other artwork from students.
- Fund raising updates and current status of fund raising goals.
- Educational issues that are current in the news or being debated — boiled down to an understandable few sentences.

Is advertising a way to go?

Why not? Unless an objection is voiced that the consensus agrees with, advertising raises extra revenue to cover the costs of the copier, computer, reduction costs, photo-developing, and colored or better-quality paper — money that would ordinarily come from the PTA budget.

Potential advertisers should be supplied with information. How many people potentially read the newsletter? How many copies are printed and distributed each issue? What are some of the articles and features of the paper? Is it possible to get a sample issue? Leave each person you talk to a sheet of paper with neatly printed answers to these questions, as well as the name and phone number of a contact person.

Also leave a rate sheet for various sizes of ads, instructions concerning the format for submitted ads, and let potential advertisers know whether the newsletter can provide artwork. And if the newsletter has any policy that may cause an ad to be rejected, state the policy on the rate sheet.

The possible advertisers can come from several sources:

- **Local businesses.** Ask the candy store around the corner, the diner, the book store, pharmacy, and grocery store to buy some advertising space in the newsletter.

- **Parents.** Many parents are professionals, with skills. A parent often needs a lawyer, for example, and in reading the newsletter sees legal services offered by a fellow parent. The lawyer/parent offers the advantages of understanding the stresses of being a parent, and the commonality of having children in the same school.

- **Child-related services.** Approach a mail-order book club, gym, dance, and exercise classes, and stores that carry videos for children.

- **Child-parent magazines.** Several dozen magazines are published for the child and/or parent. These publishers often place small ads in other papers.

- **Cultural organizations.** A children's museum, theater ensemble, or performance group.

The presentation of the newsletter speaks a thousand words

Make your newsletter readable, neat, professional and catchy. You want people to really read it, but it's got to get their attention first. Ask a parent to help out, one who's familiar with desktop publishing programs and can format the newsletter to look great, with snappy presentations of information. Produce sufficient copies to get one home to the family of each child, teachers, counselors, principals, staff, and community members.

Some parents might have access to a copy machine, especially one that can easily duplicate the hundreds of copies you'll want each issue. Ask the Class Parents to look through their lists and see if someone has volunteered that service.

Every issue of the newsletter should:
- Have a logo, and/or name, like the *Main Street Elementary Gazette*.
- Include the name, address and phone number of the PTA and of a contact person representing the PTA.
- Have a masthead, listing editor, writers, typist, etc.
- Have an issue number and date of publication.
- Be printed on brightly-colored, eye-catching paper.
- Include artwork and photos, graphics, different printing fonts, and clip art.
- Be distributed at the end of the day. Children read it first and share it at home with their parents. Make it a family event.

Designing an Effective Flyer

There are few schools or groups that don't need to put out flyers to bring people in for events like workshops, fairs, assemblies, and bake sales. And in schools that regularly hold these events, flyers are distributed several times each month. Here are some tips on making flyers that effectively bring people to an event.

Quick! You've got ten seconds. That's about how long most people devote to reading a flyer. What you're saying has to grab them right away.

Determine who the flyer is geared toward. Do you want children to come? Or is the event more for grown-ups? What languages are represented? What are you selling?

Make it so interesting that the kids read it, too. If the children look at the flyer and like what they see, they'll want to share it with their parents. Include artwork, colors, interesting lettering, and eye-catchers for kids.

Make an announcement on the loud speaker. If the flyer is being distributed by the school via "kid mail," (putting it in the child's backpack) make an announcement over the loud speaker, right before school is dismissed for the day.

The kids are an essential ingredient. Tell the children that the event described in the flyer is important to the school, and that they are part of the school, too. Ask the children to make sure they show the flyer to their parents. Get the children interested in the event, and make them part of the process.

Don't forget the information. In the flurry of designing a flyer, it's not unusual to forget things like the

- date
- address
- times
- admission costs, if any
- title of the event (play, fair, raffle)
- talent (speakers, stars, actors)
- child care, if any
- refreshments, if any
- other special features
- name and phone number for questions
- reply form to tear-off and return (if desired)

Keep the artwork simple. Don't go overboard on logos, designed borders, intricate scrolls or lettering. It dilutes the initial impression. Clean lines and simple artwork reproduce more clearly.

Print on brightly colored paper. Especially if a flyer is going home in the child's backpack, print it on colored paper that stands out easily among the white papers.

Three strikes — and you're in! Studies in direct mail methods say that, in most cases, if you send people information three times, they'll generally respond. So when you really want to push a special event, send out three flyers, or make three attempts (phone, email, mail, flyer, phone tree, note home) and you'll most likely have the attendance you want.

Parent Workshops

How are parent workshops useful?

A good workshop is a very valuable tool for reaching people and for making an impact on them. Workshops share information that is both theoretical and hands-on. More people get the information when it's given to a group, rather than in a time-consuming one-to-one approach. And when a group of people gets together, they often teach each other as much as a facilitator does.

The close personal interaction we find in an effective workshop situation can strengthen positive relationships between parents and the school, as well as between parents and other parents. The overall dynamic of an energetic workshop creates a memorable bank of experiences to draw on over time.

What are the drawbacks of workshops?

Most of the pitfalls have to do with logistics: Can one date fit the needs of a group of people with different time schedules and obligations? Can a parent — even one with the best of intentions — be sure of having that date or that evening free to attend a workshop? Where does attending a workshop fall on the priority lists we all set up for ourselves?

Time and attention spans are very limited for almost everyone these days. Parents are greedy for their own free time, giving it reluctantly and only to those topics and issues which they think are vital to their family. And a workshop doesn't always provide an ideal forum for sharing ideas; some issues are too sensitive or complicated and require a different more intimate format.

An effective workshop facilitator is a joy to find, especially one adept at helping people explore issues, one who's not judgmental or impatient, one who is educated and experienced in his or her field, one who has worked hard at developing strong skills in communication.

You can conduct a workshop by yourself!

Often, bringing in a professional speaker or facilitator is an energizing boost to your group. But, if your budget is limited, you can hold a very successful workshop by following these easy guidelines:

- Look at the resources already in your community. Often, groups in the community with similar interests will have speakers available to talk to your group, or to lead a workshop.
- When planning, consult the representatives of all players.
- Select topics of high priority for intended participants.
- Choose a presenter or facilitator who is a good communicator even if he or she is an amateur.
- Select activities that require active participation and result in some tangible outcome or product.
- Check community calendars and customs to determine preferred days and times, and schedule accordingly.
- Choose a location that is convenient, quiet, and compatible.
- Publicize the workshop in creative ways, and give people various opportunities to hear about it.
- Do intensive outreach: personal invitations, phone calls, home visits, reminders. Tell parents to tell other parents.

- Provide child care, preferably free, or child care stipends when possible.
- Provide transportation, if possible, for those who need it, or arrange transportation stipends when possible.
- Personally greet all participants, warmly and genuinely.
- Provide name tags and other forms of introduction.
- Validate everyone's participation.
- Work closely with the presenter or facilitator in keeping the program lively and short.
- Get an evaluation from each participant.
- When possible, make a video or audio recordings to share with other parents.
- Summarize for the newsletter or at the next PTA meeting.

Convince parents to participate in workshops:

- Send home fliers that are attention-getting, fun, and informative. Email as well, when possible
- Widely publicize the event, meeting, or activity in the school newsletter and in local papers.
- Post announcements in newsletters or on bulletin boards of community forums, such as church, library, shopping centers, etc.
- Talk about the event on local call-in shows.
- Get people who are respected to attend or speak.
- Get the cooperation of local businesses and industries who may employ parents. Ask them to help with bulletins, announcements, and fliers or notices in paycheck envelopes.
- Either schedule a community-wide event, like a rally, parade, etc., to celebrate your program of activities, or participate in one that's already scheduled.

Provide workshops that are relevant to the needs of parents.

Topics for workshops and seminars run the gamut, from school-related to home-based, from academic to emotional. Survey your population and find out which topics they're most interested in exploring. Give them choices — some are listed below. Encourage the parents to come up with additional topics they'd like to know more about.

Some examples of important workshop topics are:
- Helping Children with their Homework
- AIDS
- Workshops for Single Fathers
- Death and Terminal Illness
- Discipline and Managing Everyday Conflicts
- Substance Abuse: Tobacco, Drugs and Alcohol
- Bully Behavior
- Adult Education
- Vocational Training (Children and/or their Parents)
- Job Preparedness (resumes, interviews, appropriate dress)
- Being a Single Parent
- The Home as a Learning Environment (using at-hand, home-based items to expand your child's world)
- Counteracting the Guilt that Mothers Feel Going Back to Work

7. Organizing Parent-Teacher Groups

A parent-teacher group is composed primarily of parents. These are parents who want to support their child's education and growth. They want to make an impact on the school he or she goes to, and they want to become more informed. The parent group might also invite teachers to join with them in reaching their goals with at least one teacher representative

Some of these parent groups are called PTAs or PTOs (Parent-Teacher Association or Organization). Other groups that don't include teachers are called PAs. A group might be referred to as a Booster Club, Parents in Partnership, or have another name, but the idea is one of parents working together to expand their children's chances in education.

In this unit, we look at the ways in which parent energy can be organized and pointed in positive and productive directions. We explore strategies for forming a PTA and Classroom Parent Program, and share incentives that help build membership, ideas concerning communication, and tips on running an effective and dynamic parent-group meeting.

Everyone is welcomed.

Today's children often live in a family with only one parent, or several stepparents. Some children live with their grandparents, relatives, guardians, or in a foster-care situation. In all of these situations, the adult in a parental situation can greatly benefit by becoming involved in the child's education and joining the parents' group. If this group is a PTA, encourage the teachers to join as well, or ask them to at least elect a representative to attend meetings and sit on the executive board.

The PTA is a driving force in the school and the family.

With a national enrollment of 6.6 million people the PTA can be an effective, positive force in the life of a family. Some benefits to the family are that the parent group or PTA:

- Creates connections with other people.
- Helps parents learn ways of assisting their children with homework.
- Allows children to experience a sense of pride because their parents take an interest in their school.
- Exposes parents to alternative ways of parenting and learning.
- Offers parenting and communication skills.
- Gives parents hands-on experiences that build self-esteem and confidence.
- Helps parents meet people (including other parents) who can become friends and resources.
- Acts as an arsenal of knowledge and strength.
- Advocates for education and school system issues.
- Builds strong skills in leadership, decision making, negotiation, positive communication, and conflict resolution.
- Opens possible avenues to new or better employment.
- May lead to improved family life.

The PTA is an integral part of the community.

The PTA is comprised of parents. Parents are part of the community, and the community works directly with the children. The circle of people surrounding the child continues to grow when all the players on this team collaborate.

The community benefits when the PTA:

- Is a central resource for parent training, community meetings, and neighborhood events.
- Takes an active part in informing parents and community members about vital issues, such as child safety, conflict-resolution, AIDS, and other health issues.
- Organizes new programs for students, parents, and community members, like ESL and GED classes.
- Advocates for the rights of children.
- Takes part in community groups and school-board committees.
- Organizes groups of parents, students, and teachers to work with community groups in completing projects, such as a new playground or a fund raiser for a community center.

The business community gets the benefits when the PTA:

- Creates new networks of community groups, businesses, and children, and focuses on a plan of action that involves and improves programs for their future employees and consumers — the children.
- Informs and enlightens local businesses about what children need from them and ways they can work together, such as in the creation of professional mentor programs or the provision of full or partial scholarships or internships.
- Gives business a variety of options they can use to show children what professional avenues are open to them when they apply themselves to getting a rich education.

How to Form a PTA or Parent Group

PTA's and parent groups are formed in essentially the same way. Ideally, both have a strong, positive commitment to fostering communication among parents in the group and to promoting consistent individual and collective efforts toward improving educational standards.

- **Select the leadership.** Officers should include a Chairperson, President or two Co-Presidents, along with one or two Vice Presidents, a Secretary, a Treasurer, and three to four Members-at-Large.

- **Target needs and form committees to meet those needs.** Each group has its needs. These might range from grounds improvement to a painted lunchroom, ESL classes for parents to an art class for the upper grades. Find people not only willing to serve on the committee, but enthusiastic and (if possible) professionally prepared to be of some real help. Some additional committee suggestions are:
    —Membership
    —Multi-Cultural
    —Community Outreach
    —Fund-raising
    —Parent Involvement
    —Child Care
    —Parents Room
    —Nominating
    —Nutrition
    —Curriculum

- —After-school Program
- —Parent Education
- —Events Planning
- —Newsletter
- —Refreshments
- —Budget
- —By-laws
- —Discipline

- **Plan the calendar.** Decide what events the parents' group is sponsoring throughout the year, what the scheduled dates are, and distribute a calendar of these events to the school body.

- **Invite membership.** Using ways that target your particular parent group, bring people into the fold. Send out letters, email, bring in parents by holding different events. Call potential members through a telephone tree. Do a parent survey and see whom you have. Ask respondents what they want from you.

- **Involve the parents.** Pair the parents' skills with the needs of the students and the teachers. Be clever in matching talents, time constraints, and personalities. Validate members in sensitive and caring ways.

How to Bring in New Members

A PTA or parent group is only as good as its membership. A classroom and school are made of unique and special individuals, each with his own ideas and her own viewpoints. So it is with a PTA. The more parents are involved and active, the more strength and positive potential the group has.

- **Conduct a school-wide membership drive.** Start early in the fall. Put special effort into recruiting parents of kindergarten students and others who are new to the school.
    - Offer incentives to the classes bringing in the most new members.
    - Send home a packet with a flyer, a membership envelope, a letter from the principal, a handbook of the school, and any PTA information that's pertinent, like phone numbers for important contacts.
    - Distribute flyers to parents on the school grounds.
    - Set up a PTA table on a regular basis. Have posters about the PTA membership drive on bulletin boards.
    - Attach membership envelopes to the emergency cards sent home to the parents by the school.
- **Invite parents and teachers to a "Fall Membership Harvest Breakfast."** In the teachers' lounge or parents' room, serve coffee, juice and a variety of pastries and fruit, or choose other food items

appealing to the cultures of your parents. Supply name tags for parent's name, child's name and classroom number. Give a brief informal opening speech, and encourage people to meet and talk to one another, using any one of a number of ice-breaker activities.

- **Find class parents.** Every class needs at least one parent who can act as a liaison to the PTA, bringing information from the classroom to the PTA and vice versa. The class parent helps to organize events and trips in each class, prints or helps to work on the class newsletter, helps with tutoring, collects names and phone numbers for the class list, and, most importantly, inspires other parents to become more involved in their child's education.

- **Poster contest.** Organize a school-wide poster contest. Tell the children what aspects of the PTA are important, and why, via a flyer home. Then ask them to make a poster that emphasizes these aspects.

- **Talk to the teachers.** Ask them to share PTA information at parent-teacher conferences. Get them to work directly with parents to convince them that getting involved in the PTA is a vital step in the right direction.

- **Principal letter.** Ask the principal to send a letter home, recommending that the parents become more involved in the PTA.

YOUR PTA
123 Main St.
Your Town, USA

September 1st

Dear Parent,

The school year has begun. Our goal in this new year is to involve you even more in your child's school. You and your child are both very valuable members of our school community.

We invite you to become a member of the Parent-Teacher Association. Why? Because the more you are involved in your child's education, the better chance your child has to succeed. The more you know about how your child is growing and learning, the more effective the teachers and the principal can be. Your help makes a surprisingly big difference.

When you become a member of the PTA, you get a lot in return:
- A school newsletter keeping you up to date with school news.
- Information on children's rights and parents' rights.
- Current tips on homework help, communication skills, and information pertinent to raising children in today's world.
- An opportunity to meet other parents, to make new friends, to enlarge your parent and professional network.
- Guidelines for getting more involved in decision making within the school and the school district.
- Membership opportunities in other local and national parent groups and organizations.

The PTA dues you pay are not mandatory and small compared to the big picture. With your contribution the PTA pays for important events and added school features, such as after-school programs, parent classes, class trips, teacher salaries, literature and textbooks, and special events.

Join us, won't you? Take your place in a group of parents, just like you, who want one thing for their child: the BEST ! Our first PTA meeting is _____ . We really look forward to seeing you there !

Sincerely yours,

Rosemary Gomez, PTA President

Organize a Classroom Parent Program

A Class Parent Program = Parent Power

Each class is a unit unto itself. Together, the classes form another unit called the school. When each class has at least one parent representative, called a Class Parent, the school is well represented, and each class has a loud and clear voice.

The Class Parents Program (CPP) serves a wide variety of functions. It:

- Reaches fellow parents and makes a strong connection with them.

- Finds out parents' and students' needs and works on innovative ways to fill them.

- Strengthens the bonds between the family and the school.

- Informs parents about events in the classroom and ways the parents can take part: attending parent-teacher conferences; helping with class trips or parties; creating and supervising art, drama, and music projects; helping out other families in times of crisis; speaking, storytelling, and tutoring.

- Gives information to parents and students about school-based events and opportunities, such as family workshops, PTA meetings, and raffles.

- Works with parents in areas vital to improved family relations and self-help, like parenting and communication workshops, and seminars on discipline, health, and nutrition issues.

- Acts as a resource center for information valuable to parents, developing networks into the community's available resources, such as the identity of good tutors, how to get a child into special classes, etc.

A Class Parent Program is a win/win for everyone.

When parents involve themselves in a CPP, they learn and grow along the way.

Parents can:

- Develop hands-on skills in decision making and leadership.
- Learn tips from other parents, in communication, patience, humor, and practical advice geared to improving parenting skills.
- Enlarge their sphere of interests
- Help, and be helped by, the PTA or parents' group.

How do we start a Class Parent Program?

The first essential step is to get the commitment from the principal, the teachers, and the PTA or parents' group. They all give their support and can advise you about ways that you can launch a CPP.

The next steps are to:

- **Select a Chairperson.** At the inception of the CPP, select a supervising coordinator from the Executive Board of the PTA or parents' group.
- **Talk to each individual teacher.** Ask her or him to recommend a parent (or two, or three) who might be a candidate for the CPP. The parent should be one who is involved, interested in the children of the class, and one with some available time during the day.
- **Make a plan of action.** Come up with a rough plan of action, one that, at least initially, makes sense and that you can share with Class Parent candidates. The plan should include some events the CPP can begin in each classroom, like:

- —A class newsletter
- —A class logo or motto
- —A good routine for handling birthday parties
- —Regular tips for parents on homework, communication, discipline, conflict resolution, bullying, parenting skills, etc.

- **Contact the parent.** Ask if she or he is willing to be the Class Parent. Discuss the plan of action, above, as well as plans to hold CPP regular meetings. If the parent agrees, ask him or her to come up with suggestions for class activities and other ways the CPP can help.

- **Work with the Class Parents.** Give them ways to contact and associate with other parents, like the telephone tree or through email. Make up a CPP Kit in which you show them sample newsletters, a letter to parents, requests for volunteers, and parent surveys. Ask them for other suggestions and encourage active participation.

- **Hold regular meetings.** Designate a regular morning, afternoon and/or evening each month, like the third Thursday night, to be the CPP meeting. Hold the meeting at the school or in someone's home. Discuss the various activities that the Class Parents have supervised or organized. State some of the pitfalls, and ask for solutions or advice. Come up with a long-range plan of action or goal.

- **Connect with the PTA or parent group.** Send regular reports to the PTA about what's happening with the CPP. Make sure reports are included in the school newsletter.

Forming a Telephone Tree

A Telephone Tree is a fast and efficient way of passing information among parents. It takes just a few moments to spread the word. A Telephone Tree can give information out, and bring information back in. And, it's an important way of involving parents who are really busy and can't do much but who want to contribute.

The Telephone Tree below reaches 30 people, which should cover most class sizes. If you can involve more people in the calls, you can lessen the number of calls each person needs to make. And if you need to cover a larger number of callers, increase your starter numbers, or ask each person to call ten people rather than five. Make sure you mention to the callers that the phone numbers are confidential and used only for class business.

- **Get the phone numbers and names of the children.** Talk to the class parent and get the class list, if one exists, with phone numbers and names of the children and their parents.

- **Get 5 "starter parents."** Ask 5 parents to volunteer to start the telephone tree. Provide them with the information they will need to give out, or gather.

- **The 5 parents each call another 5 parents.** Give each of the 5 parents the names and phone numbers of 5 other parents. Ask them to make the calls.

Incentives for Joining a Parent Group

Not everyone jumps on the bandwagon of involvement right away. It takes time to get people's interests, and then it takes more time to get their commitment. It takes additional time to get them to live up to that commitment. And it takes even more time to get these parents to commit to staying committed...! So be patient. And don't resist stooping to bribery. Sometimes that's just what it takes. Here are some suggestions:

- **Cash.** At some of the regularly-scheduled PTA meetings, have a door prize, and award cash or a gift certificate to the winner.

- **Class prizes.** For the class that brings in the most new members, and/or the most renewals of membership, offer a prize: A pizza party, an ice cream party, a special field trip.

- **Discounts.** Talk to local merchants, such as grocery stores, clothing stores, department stores, or movie theaters, and see if they will sponsor discounts for PTA members. They get free publicity and increased community exposure. Everyone involved wins.

- **Books.** Offer free bookstore gift cards for children, or adults, as a bonus for membership drives. When people make contributions to the PTA above $25, or as door prizes, books are a great prize.

- **Information.** With new memberships, give out school handbooks, a national PTA handbook, curriculum handbook, school pin, or an autograph book, mug, or T-shirt with the school logo and colors.

- **Movie tickets.** With the help of a local movie theater that will either donate or sell discount tickets, offer a free movie ticket to each parent or family that comes to the meetings.

- **Door prizes.** Have a drawing at every meeting. Offer 2 to 5 prizes for each drawing, donated by local merchants. A turkey at Thanksgiving, a gift certificate for the December holidays, or candy for Easter or Passover. Your choices are endless.

How to Conduct a Parent Group Meeting

Each group has a personality, and a way of working

The same applies to the way in which the group conducts its meetings. Some groups may choose to follow strict parliamentary procedure; other groups are more informal, with few rules. The person conducting the meeting, however, can benefit from **a few all-purpose pointers...**

- **Keep it informal.** Although you want to keep the meeting in line, you also want it to be cordial, with an air of informality that welcomes parents and teachers and doesn't scare them off. Greet people warmly and by name when possible as they walk into the meeting.

- **Keep it brief.** Whether you have one issue to cover or quite a few, remember that each one needs a discussion, pros and cons, and often requires a vote. Try to move things along. If discussions veer off track, tell those involved that the peripheral issue can be discussed at another time, or that the person wanting to see some action taken can begin researching the process and bring information back to the next meeting. Make an agenda, distribute it, and stick to it. *Start the meeting on time.*

- **Keep it friendly.** In almost every group, there are parents who are angrier or more antagonistic than others. They can easily upset a positive mood or change the tenor of a meeting with their emotions. Do your best to directly address people

Try to be one of the people on whom nothing is lost.
—Henry James

who are being emotional, and suggest that perhaps they speak with you alone, or that they pose a solution to the problem at hand, rather than simply concentrating on the problem. Ask them to put the solution in writing and to submit a plan of action to the executive board. Suggest an ad hoc committee be formed and that they chair that group. Keep your sense of humor. You'll need it more than almost any other quality.

- **Keep the rules and by-laws posted.** Whether you have a PTA, a PA, or another kind of parents' group, make sure that you have a visible parents' bulletin board on which the by-laws can be posted.

- **Keep it fair.** Everyone is equal, and each person represents at least one child. Only one person gets the floor at a time. Make sure there are translators for people whose English is poor. The leader of the meeting doesn't favor friends or refuse to let a possibly rival faction speak. Be courteous. Let others speak, and don't hog the floor. Don't allow personality issues to come into a meeting. Make parent meetings win-win experiences.

- **Keep the members informed.** Give people advance notice of the meeting. Take accurate minutes and make them available. Be open to getting phone calls or talking to people after the meeting.

8. Forty-five Ways to Reward Volunteers
Those Two Magic Words: "Thank You!"

Parents, people, children, adults, old, young — everyone needs an occasional "thank you." When we work hard, we like to be thanked, to be shown that our contributions are noticed, and appreciated. We like people to care for us.

To stay involved in any effort — but especially in a parent involvement program — a person needs to be recognized, needs to be thanked, and needs to know that she or he is making a tangible difference with his or her efforts in the lives of children.

Here are 45 ways to show your thanks and appreciation:

1. A personal thank-you note, with a real signature, not a stamp.
2. Recognition in a newsletter or school newspaper.
3. Send a birthday card.
4. Show the person genuine respect all the time.
5. Be a good listener.
6. Smile — directly at the individual.
7. Greet people by name.
8. Take time — to explain, to listen, to support.
9. Lead regular rap sessions or support groups.
10. Provide child-care during volunteer time whenever possible.
11. Give people more responsibility.
12. Write a letter of recognition for a perspective employer.
13. Use people — when appropriate — as consultants.

14. Place a suggestion box near volunteer headquarters.
15. Whenever possible, provide beverages/snacks.
16. On Thanksgiving Day, send the family a card sharing your thanks for the help and time given by the family member.
17. Promptly reimburse expenses.
18. Arrange a theater party, with (discounted) tickets and dinner at a restaurant (one that is willing to provide a group rate).
19. Respect individual sensitivities.
20. Praise the person highly to friends, employers, and others close to him or her.
21. Make working conditions volunteer-friendly.
22. Instigate a VIP program (Volunteer Involvement Program) where each week or month, a volunteer is recognized: his or her face and/or brief biography is printed in a newsletter or newspaper, accomplishments described, and genuine thanks and appreciation given. Award a dinner for two donated by a neighborhood restaurant whose generosity is also acknowledged.
23. Respect everyone as a unique being, with skills and talents, and with foibles and human faults. Accept the whole package.
24. Keep an updated file on each volunteer. Include name and address; child's name, class, and address if different from parent; work and home numbers; volunteered skills and talents; and best times to contact.
25. Have regular volunteer staff meetings with brainstorming and idea swaps.
26. Give recognition teas or a light breakfast.
27. Help build people's self-confidence, self-esteem and leadership skills.
28. Provide the best training you can to help people do their job well.
29. Send letters to public figures commending the volunteer's accomplishments.

30. Award plaques and documents, in a ceremony when possible.
31. Understand that they — like you — have a personal life.
32. Honor the time and privacy that having a family demands. Don't take advantage of volunteers.
33. Ask people to evaluate you regularly. Listen to their evaluations. Act.
34. Say "Good morning," "good afternoon," "good night," and "thank you.
35. Think carefully of the suitability of each volunteer to each job. Make sure the volunteer and the job are well matched.
36. Ask for suggestions when deciding or voting on policy matters.
37. Plan surprise celebrations: an impromptu party, an "Everybody's Birthday" party, or cake and champagne. Sometimes just plug in a pot of coffee and open a box of cookies.
38. Set up a scholarship fund. Send some of your volunteers to special workshops, or to adult education and management classes.
39. Give volunteers safe working conditions. Make sure that rooms are ventilated, warm, and safe, with water and hygienic facilities.
40. Even though the volunteers may work under you or with your supervision, be real with them. Be yourself.
41. Find ways of getting various discounts for your group.
42. Offer positive challenges to the group as a whole and to individuals.
43. Don't confuse the group as a whole with the individuals in it.
44. Organize a picnic and softball game, or a teachers vs. parents indoor volleyball game in winter.
45. Always defend your volunteers. Stand up for them and behind them.

Section Three
Parents Reach Out: To the School, the Community, and Each Other

This may be the last section, but it's certainly not the least! In fact, this is the most important section of all three in *The Do's and Don'ts of Parent Involvement*.

Why is it so important? Because this section is dedicated to those people who have really connected with an idea: that an involved parent is essential for any genuine growth to happen in a child. And because these people want other parents to share in the knowledge and experience and fun they've gotten out of their involvement. They want educators, administrators, community groups, and other interested individuals to see that the impact this involvement makes on a child is measurable and dramatic.

Parent involvement works in wondrous ways...

Parent involvement is effective and exciting when parents become so involved that they want to reach out to other parents.

Parents who reach out to others have already made their own decision to get involved. They want to do something, however small, that can improve their chances of working successfully with their children. They know they can make a real difference. Now, the next step is to bring other parents into the process.

Parent involvement takes many forms. Some of the basic and most traditional levels of parent involvement are:

- **Responsible parenting.** Parents who guide a child in learning and in social growth at home, and who send a child to school fed, rested, feeling positive and loved.

- **Home teaching.** At home, parents who help with homework and class projects, and are active in parent-teacher collaboration.

- **Attending.** Parents who come to school events, like plays and assemblies, and show appreciation and support.

- **Assisting.** On a volunteer or salaried basis, parents who work in the class as an aide, tutor, or paraprofessional, or in the school's office.

- **Making decisions.** Parents who serve on a committee or board, such as the principal selection committee or local school board. Also, parents involved in school-based work, such as volunteering for the parents' and teachers' advisory council, or running for a PTA executive office.

- **Adult learning.** Parents who take part in workshops and seminars sponsored by the school or parents' group, where they learn about parenting and improve various skills. Also, parents who enroll in adult education classes such as ESOL. or GED

- **Advocating.** As representatives of their school, neighborhood, and/or community, these parents speak to politicians, business leaders, and other decision-makers about the school and its needs.

The Children Are the Focus
Our Children Are the Connection

Most parents struggle to find the special time and energy needed to love, nurture, and guide their own children. It's even more difficult to share their skills and time with children who aren't their own. But our children are all connected. Children share ideas with one another, they nourish and support each other, and they can be each other's best teachers. Children exert an enormous influence over one another. All children need and deserve our attention, our skills — and our love.

We are all part of the global village

Find an extra hour or two, and consider ways you can give your time to other children. The reward at the end? The knowledge that you are improving the well-being of the children receiving your attention. *You're making a difference.*

It takes a whole village to raise a child
—African proverb

- **Volunteer to work with a class that's not your own child's.** If you have a talent or an interest that you can share with children, ask the principal if he or she can suggest a class, other than your child's class, to speak to.

- **Conduct a fund raiser for the whole school.** Spearhead a raffle. Organize an auction, like a silent auction or arts and crafts auction. Or, ask the principal if she or he has any fund raising ideas that you can implement for the school.

- **Be a Big Brother or Big Sister.** There may be children in your child's school who need a good listener, a mentor, or simply a caring adult friend. Ask the school counselor if he or she knows of such a child. Find out about the child's educational background from the teacher. Ask if the teacher thinks the child can use tutoring, your individual skills, or just talking and listening.

Parents Are Valuable Resources

Parents can show teachers the best way to reach other parents

Parents can create a positive, far-reaching circle when they work together with teachers. This can show teachers the most effective ways of reaching other parents. Parents can give teachers very practical hands-on ideas for making other parents part of their children's education.

Ignite the teacher's interests

When parents work closely with teachers, the collaboration can produce stimulating materials on improving homework, communication skills, and parenting skills, as well as guidance on talking to children about bullying, drugs, discipline, health issues, and sex.

Parents work with a teacher liaison

In most school systems and districts, a teacher or staff member acts as a liaison between community members, parents, and school staff. She or he interacts with families, community members, and agencies. This liaison position compares with any specialist's position, and requires a welcoming work space, prep time, ongoing access to information, and available training. This is generally a paid position.

Parents and teachers can research budgets

Often, parents can be a valuable resource in helping teachers find out about funding for which they might qualify. This can be grant money, special funds, or normal budget lines they never received. Monies can come from the city, state or federal government, and they can also come from the private sector.

But it takes research, and it takes time to look for sources, as well as to write proposals and fill out the many forms usually involved. Follow-up is equally important in making sure that the agencies involved are paying attention to proposals and requests.

Budget allocations are usually made for:
- Staff development and teacher training that give teachers and staff sharpened skills and awareness about working closely with families.

- Development of home learning materials that support the teacher's curriculum and educational goals.

Ways That Parents Can Reach Out to Teachers

Parents can be an asset in the classroom

Very few parents are controlling, manipulative, or destructive in the classroom environment, but those who do behave this way can create a wrong impression about the constructive and contributing parents who do so much to enrich classrooms and schools.

Some teachers may be reluctant to let parents into the classroom, except on a limited basis, much less encourage parents to augment their curriculum and teaching methods. But parents and teachers who learn to work in collaboration can elevate a classroom in every way.

Parents who want to connect more strongly and earnestly with teachers can try some of the following strategies to get their point across:

- **Teacher-of-the-Month Awards.** Every month, a teachers is chosen by the parents and honored for his or her special qualities. Criteria for selection might be something like: The Teacher who... ...has the best smile; ...gives the most creative homework; ...demonstrates respect for the students; ...takes the kids on the most fun field trips; etc. Display a photo of the honored teacher on a central bulletin board with captions.

- **A Once-a-Month Teacher's Day.** On the same day each month (like the second Monday, or the third Thursday), the parents encourage one another to do something honoring their child's teacher. It can be a note of validation, a donation of time or skills, giving the teacher an item he or she can use in the classroom — or a well-polished apple!

- **Class Parent.** Volunteer to be a Class Parent (see Section Two). Various forms of assistance include being a tutor; a chaperone on trips; driving small groups of students to special events; photocopying; or helping the teacher and other parents with student birthday parties, holiday celebrations, and special days.

- **Print materials.** Parents with facilities and skills can help augment the teacher's classroom needs with items like a class newspaper, test papers, pre-printed homework assignments, and information lists.

- **Audio/Visual.** Organize film or video rentals and their showings. Organize class photos and photographic displays. Develop film. Videotape class events like plays, spelling contests, performances, and experiments.

We all need to hear "I appreciate"

Teachers are very human. Like all of us, they need to hear the words *thank you*. They need a pat on the back and to know that you've seen what they've done to make your child's life fuller.

Find ways to say thanks to your child's teacher, or teachers. Let them know you're aware that their job is a challenging one. Let them know when they've really succeeded at getting through to your child, and let them know that you've seen it happen. Describe to teachers some of the ways in which your child is changing.

The seeds take a while to bloom

Like anything worth doing right, it usually takes time. Teaching is a process, one that's composed of small deeds and baby steps. Often, a teacher has no idea if anything she or he has done has "taken hold." Many teachers tell of students returning to them years later with stories of how they affected the student. Sometimes the teacher only remembers that child as difficult, recalcitrant, or unbending, and despaired of ever being able to affect the student. Yet the teacher did get through!

Teachers are challenged by this constant worry. Am I making a real difference in this student's life? Am I getting my knowledge across to my class? Am I preparing them for the harder grades ahead? Am I yelling too much? Am I giving the proper perspective on a subject? Do I feel genuine concern ? Do I show respect?

Your child's teacher needs your approval

Obviously, the teacher can succeed without your approval, but it's a lot harder to tackle the job of teaching without support. Your approval can be truly genuine if you ask yourself a few questions about your child's teacher.

Ask yourself these questions:
- Do I think that the teacher has taken a real and on-going interest in my child?
- Has my child shown substantial growth in mastering subjects like reading, writing, math, science, music, art, sports?
- Does the teacher foster a sense of creativity in my child, which evidences itself in many ways?
- Does he or she encourage positive discipline and self-control? Have my child's self-esteem and maturity increased?
- Does he or she keep me informed regularly about my child and the class?
- Does he or she encourage me to take part in the classroom and offer me a variety of choices concerning how I can help?
- Is my child prone to being troublesome in class? If so, is the teacher dealing well with that fact?

If you've answered 'yes' to most of these questions, your child's teacher deserves a note of appreciation, a phone call, or another creative "thank you."

Ways That Parents Can Reach Out to Each Other

Parents Live Challenging Lives

Today's parents live with stress, worries, economic hardships, and fear of physical violence. In addition, they are responsible for the mental, physical, emotional, and economic well-being of their children. The end result is a parent who often feels inadequate and overwhelmed by the job of parenting.

Too often, perfectly reasonable adults can lose their objectivity as parents. Very few solid role models show them how to be successful parents. An occasional parent fails miserably. Others are sure that they're parenting badly, though actually they're not. Few parents believe in themselves or view their parenting abilities objectively.

We who are parents need each other. We can also benefit one another with our experiences, viewpoints, ideas, and suggestions. But many parents are ashamed about sharing their private problems or asking questions. It's hard to admit that we feel insecure about an area we're supposed to have mastered: parenting. We need to assure one another that parenting is an ongoing process. We need to share a thousand different ways to help each other survive — and thrive!

When parents come together with positive energy and a commitment to helping all children, not just our own, a lot gets done — and a lot of problems get solved along the way.

Keep it simple

Often, the simplest and most direct approaches — like those that follow — are the most effective. Whenever possible, involve your child, too. Let the child see your values and work ethics in action. Enjoy the rewards of working together, side by side, creating new friendships and accomplishing positive results.

- **Start a parents' group.** If no good groups exist, start one. Talk to parents in the park or at school, at church or in the supermarkets, at your job or in the community center. Involve them in getting together to meet one another and to share common experiences. Place an ad in a community newsletter asking for interested people to call you. Make flyers and put them on bulletin boards in supermarkets, apartment lobbies, schools, places of worship, video stores, libraries, community centers, and doctors' offices.

- **Join an existing group.** Many groups now exist nationally as well as on a local level that support a vast number of issues, from single parenting to step-parenting. Look in the phone book. Call your church or community center for times and addresses.

- **Get together with one or more parents regularly.** Even if it's only an hour a week for coffee and cake, make a date and schedule that you keep on a regular basis. Alternate locations from home to home, or meet in a coffee shop. When you can, get together without children for a needed break or some adult conversation.

- **Organize a community project.** Work together with a community center, church, or school, and organize a project that benefits the parents and children of the community. Design, raise funds for, and build a playground. Clean up a city block or beautify a stretch of rural highway.

- **Help out your neighbors.** When a fellow parent is ill or in crisis, respond in ways you think will be helpful: shopping, baby-sitting, cooking, chores, comfort, transportation to doctors. Enlist the help and support of other parents when the situation warrants. Especially in times of crisis, fellow parents can be very soothing and supportive.

- **Look for "surrogate parents" and Big Brothers/Sisters.** People who don't have children of their own, by choice or by circumstance, are often excellent resources. They can help a child with tutoring and encouragement. They can coach sports after school, form Big Brother or Big Sister relationships, act as professional mentors, and provide strong emotional support.

- **Help parents with their own education.** Many parents lack the necessary skills, degrees, or qualifications that can help them advance to a better job, with higher pay and better benefits. Organize classes for parents, such as ESL or GED sessions. Enlist the help of a local college, high school, church, or community group — or start such classes as a joint effort between the school and local organizations. Put out flyers. Make phone calls. Have some of the more outgoing parents contact parents who are shy or reticent and tell them about the classes.

- **Help parents with their careers.** Research various professionals who can conduct regular classes or seminars in vocational training, counseling, showing parents ways of looking at career options and vocational alternatives.

- **Parents can tutor parents.** On either a volunteer basis, or for a small stipend, parents from the community can be trained to be tutors for other parents. Tutoring can be ESL or GED-related, or can be specific to subjects they're studying. Parents can also tutor parents in homework skills, conflict resolution, role playing, and parenting skills.

- **Organize a health and nutrition center.** Unlike a medical center, a preventative health center works with parents in nutrition, good diet, exercise, and other steps they can take to prevent health problems. When parents work together and with their children, the school's absentee rate goes down and the students are more receptive to learning and excelling.

Asking Parents to Give

Money was available — once upon a time

There used to be a distinct line between what expenses the school system bore and what extras were paid for by parents. That was then — this is now.

Today's city, state, and federal budget cuts have dealt a heavy blow to most public schools. These slashed budgets come on top of a system with bulging classrooms, historically neglected and badly maintained buildings, and very few supplies, from paper to textbooks to extra equipment like computers or science equipment, and from para-professionals and arts teachers to sports programs.

Parents can turn it all around

A parent who wants the best education for his or her child needs to work for it. And work hard. Parents can contribute to a higher standard of education for their child in many ways, but primarily through fund raising, giving of time and skills, and advocacy.

Public schools stand for an ideal that is almost exclusively American: a promise of success and achievement, a diverse mixture of students reflective of the society that supports them, and the chance to interact with a cross section of people from different economic, religious, cultural, and ethnic backgrounds.

Public school is worth fighting for

Parents and children are loyal to the ideals and potential of public school education, and are increasingly dedicated to pledging their skills, creativity, money, and time to making the schools work even better.

Some schools benefit from serving more affluent parents; others suffer not only from sparse budget allocations, but from a low-income parent base as well. Parents — along with administrators and teachers — can look at school-wide use of funds, and ensure that classes which traditionally get more funding share the wealth with less privileged classes, and work toward the goal of equitable distribution of all monies raised.

Be a squeaky wheel

Parents who donate their time and skills, energy and talents, are vital to the survival of the school. They can make it thrive. And, the impact of firmly involved parents on the political system can create lasting change, as well. Writing out a check, or volunteering a few hours per semester isn't always enough. Get mad about budget cuts and do something about it. Write letters, start petitions, try to organize other parents, align yourself with organizations that are making a real difference. An hour of political action is just as valuable as selling raffle tickets. Can parents do both? In today's uncertain times, we don't have a choice any longer.

Ways That Parents Can Give

Time, creativity, skills, energy, and elbow grease

- **Fund raising:** Money can be raised for direct purchase of materials, supplies, equipment, staff salaries, events, trips, textbooks, musical instruments, after- school programs, extra programs, rooftop gardens and playgrounds, art and music programs.

- **Walk-a-thon.** Each child gets sponsors who pledge money based on the distance the child walks, like around the block several times, or down the road and back again. All the children in school participate on the same day. The event is widely touted, with food, entertainment, and T-shirts. The children are given a sticker each time they complete a round of walking, and at the end can redeem their stickers for money — which goes back to the school.

- **School Benefits.** Using a variety of themes, enlist local politicians, celebrities, and business leaders to appear and speak. Serve wine, cheese, fruit, bread, and soda. Decorate the room.

- **Raffles.** Offer good prizes, like cash, trips, airline tickets, and gift certificates donated by local merchants or parents. Have pre-printed tickets that give the date of the drawing and the prizes.

- **Read-a-thon.** Each child recruits people to sponsor each page read in a given time period; for example, in a week of reading at home or at the child's leisure. Or, hold a marathon read-in, at the school library.

- **Mail appeals.** Letters to parents, community members, and neighbors, asking for their support in donations, skills, or advice. If the school can get a celebrity or community leader to write the letter and sign it, that helps give the effort extra appeal.

- **Dinners.** Organize a large potluck dinner. Ask each person to bring a food dish or to donate supplies. Charge admission.

- **Candy sales.** Numerous companies sell candy at a discount, which the school or group re-sells at a high profit. Sales are good around holidays, like Easter, Passover, and Mother's Day.

- **Dances.** Organize a "50's Dance," a "Country-Western Hoedown," or a dance with some other theme. Hold it in the school cafeteria, or ask a local nightclub or hall to donate an evening. Charge admission and give away a door prize.

- **Auction and Dinner.** Ask for donations from parents and local businesses. These can range from movie posters to books, airline tickets to small appliances and gift certificates. Raffle off prizes like hand-made quilts, and paintings or ceramics done in art class. Ask teachers to donate their time as an auction "item;" for example, taking four kids to a museum or giving a week's worth of free tutoring. Begin the night with the auction, and end it with a simple buffet dinner which has been cooked by parents or donated by local restaurants.

- **Magic Show.** Invite local magicians, ventriloquists, slight-of-hand artists, and jugglers to come to the school. Advertise through the neighborhood, and hold the event on a Saturday or Sunday. Invite local food vendors to sell food, or ask the parents to cook.

Volunteering time

The school can cut back its personnel budget when parents volunteer to take the place of paid workers.

- **Conduct workshops for volunteers.** Organize a series of workshops that train parents to do different kinds of volunteering. Often, a volunteer can have the best of intentions, but does a mediocre or even disastrous job because he or she has not received instructions or guidance.

- **Welcome new parents.** Be part of a team that welcomes new parents into the school, conducts school tours, writes handbooks about the school, and contributes articles to local newspapers.

- **Work at the school.** Be a volunteer aide, security guard, lunchroom supervisor, before-school or after-school traffic monitor, custodial helper, cafeteria helper, or playground supervisor. Telephone the parents of absent or tardy students, work in the library, help in the computer lab, distribute mail, or assemble books for teachers, staff, and students.

- **Start a Breakfast Book Club.** Some of the children who are dropped off early by working parents thrive on the excitement of looking at books and reading them with a volunteer who listens and encourages them.

- **Science Fair volunteer.** Students who need help with their science fair project benefit from the help of volunteers who can work closely with them, helping to construct the project at school.

- **Clean the classroom.** Gather a group of parents together and, before school starts, clean, paint, and organize alongside the teacher or custodian. The collaborative efforts create a positive start for the new school year.

- **Organize the parents' room.** Alone or with other parents, create a new environment in the parents' room. Build shelves, food cabinets, a changing table, and storage for various parent events and supplies, like books and crayons.

Donating skills

- **School library.** Help the librarian, if there is one, by sorting books, putting them back on the shelves, organizing the card files, and putting the books into a data base.

- **Tutor.** Work with the principal's office and find children who can flourish when given extra time in math, reading, science, or computer skills. Give those children 1 to 3 hours a week.

- **Curriculum committee.** Create or join a committee that advises and oversees curriculum decisions.

- **Writers' workshop.** One afternoon per week, conduct a writers workshop for interested students. Meet in the school library, parents room, or at your home.

- **Recruitment.** Make forays into the neighborhoods around the school. Talk to preschools and day-care centers about the benefits of your school. Create and distribute flyers that talk about the school and provide a schedule of tours for potential students and parents.

- **Office work.** Talk to the principal about filling in for the secretary. Help with phones, filing, sorting, and organizing.

- **Lobbying.** Talk frequently with local politicians and businesses. Give them the high points of the school. Talk about your unique population. Ask for their help in hearing about and applying for grants, and getting public forums and community support. Also:
    —Meet with the city council member.
    —Appeal to private foundations.
    —Talk to local businesses.
    —Meet with community members and agencies.

Concluding Remarks

The Do's and Don'ts of Parent Involvement is a reflection of the energies and solutions volunteered by many parents across the country. It is our sincerest hope that these collective thoughts can be of value to other parents, schools, and community groups, and that you'll provide us with feedback at info@InnerchoicePublishing.com

If your heart is in Social-Emotional Learning, visit us online.

Come see us at
www.InnerchoicePublishing.com

Our web site gives you a look at all our other Social-Emotional Learning-based books, free activities, articles, research, and learning and teaching strategies. Every week you'll get a new Sharing Circle topic and lesson.

INNERCHOICE Publishing

15079 Oak Chase Court
Wellington, FL 33414

www.ingramcontent.com/pod-product-compliance
Lightning Source LLC
Chambersburg PA
CBHW081939170426
43202CB00018B/2947